Song Lyrics in Chart Form

(in Book Form)

Erik Tanouye

ALSO BY ERIK TANOUYE:

The Lovely Breeze
A Fake Museum

WRITING AS NATHAN PONSOR:

Human Satellite

WRITING AS NATHANIEL ERICKSON:

How To Replace an Empty Roll
of Toilet Paper: An Instruction Manual

Song Lyrics
in Chart Form
(in Book Form)

ERIK TANOUYE

TO
YNS

TOYNS PUBLISHING
New York City

To purchase copies of this book in bulk, please contact us by email at the address below.

toynspublishing.tumblr.com | toynsbooks@gmail.com

If you enjoyed this book, please consider rating it online wherever you can and telling your friends about it. We love word of mouth and social media.

TOYNS Publishing, New York City

10 9 8 7 6 5 4 3 2

Copyright © 2015 Erik Tanouye

ISBN: 978-0-9970678-0-4

DEDICATION

This book is for all the music lovers in history. But especially for those people who have physically made love to music, like by trying to have sex with a record, or putting their genitals on a guitar, or licking a radio in an erotic manner, that sort of thing.

CONTENTS

Dedication   i

Contents   iii

The Charts   1

Index   175

THE CHARTS

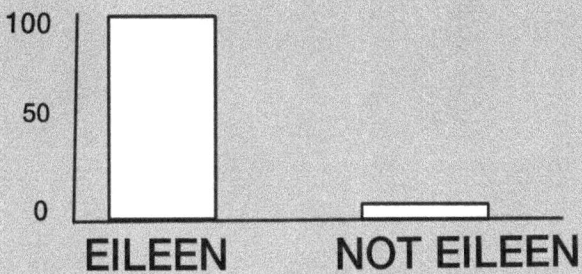

People Who Should Come On

EILEEN   NOT EILEEN

Source: Dexy's Midnight Runners

1

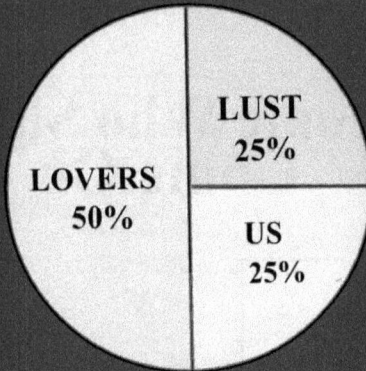

This song is a collaboration between Bruce Springsteen and Patti Smith, who met when they were both shopping for sweaty white t-shirts at the same thrift store in New Jersey.

Depth of Bad

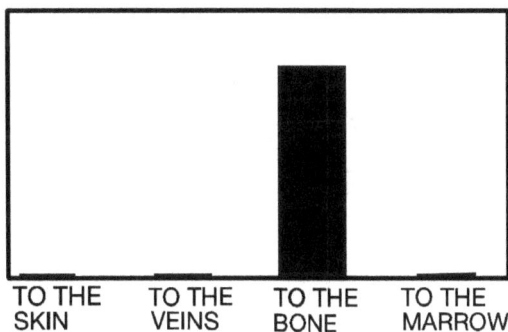

| TO THE SKIN | TO THE VEINS | TO THE BONE | TO THE MARROW |

Source: George Thorogood & The Destroyers

Being "Bad to the Bone" is not covered by most health insurance plans unless you have a tattoo to prove your condition.

Best Methods of Transportation when on The Wild Side

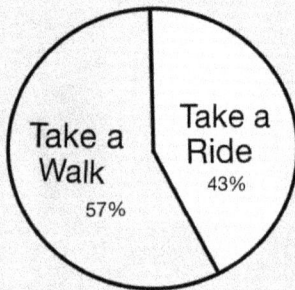

Take a Walk 57%

Take a Ride 43%

Source: Lou Reed, Mötley Crüe

Lou Reed's "A Walk on the Wild Side" took its title from Nelson Algren's novel about New Orleans, although its lyrics refer to real-life characters from Andy Warhol's Factory art scene in New York City.

The Mötley Crüe song is probably based on something that happened at a strip club.

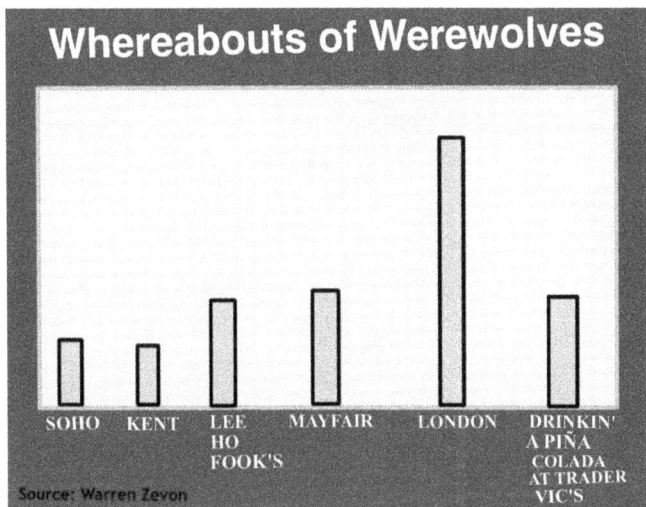

Whereabouts of Werewolves

SOHO KENT LEE HO FOOK'S MAYFAIR LONDON DRINKIN' A PIÑA COLADA AT TRADER VIC'S

Source: Warren Zevon

Although we call them werewolves in America, in London they are known as werewoulves.

TYPE OF PRECIPITATION

| Rain | Sleet | Snow | Men |

Sources: Paul Jabara, Paul Shaffer, The Weather Girls

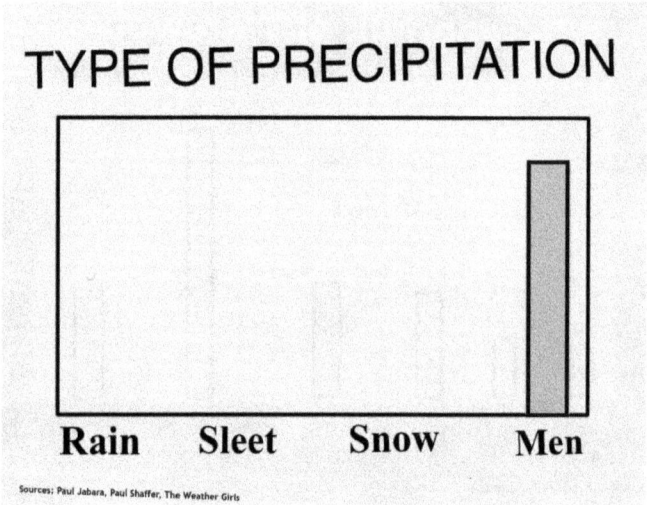

Most meteorologists agree that it would be impossible for men to rain down from the sky. But most meteorologists al-don't believe in love.

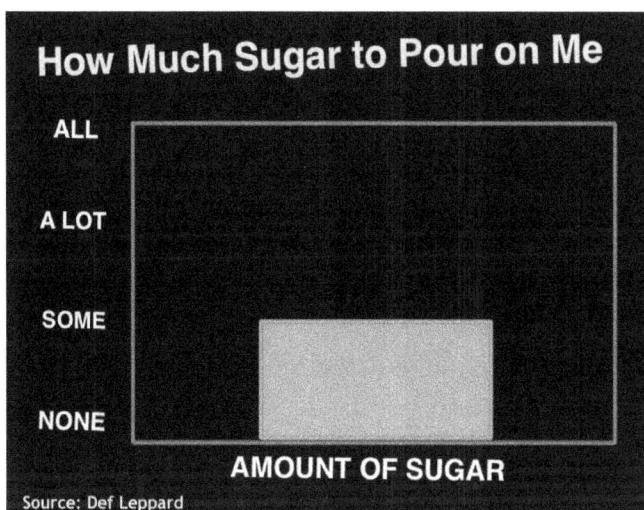

In 1995, it took Def Leppard drummer Rick Allen twice as long to pour sugar on things as his bandmates. Not because he was missing an arm, but because he was busy pleading guilty to charges of spousal abuse and was distracted from his sugar pouring.

A List of Reasons
Why I've Gotta Be So Rude

Source: MAGIC!

1. You arrived at my home unannounced
   and started knocking on my door,
   waking me up early on Saturday morning
2. You drive recklessly
   (speeding, in your own words, "like a jet")
3. Your plan to kidnap my daughter, taking
   her to "another galaxy," shows an alarming
   lack of understanding of her ability to survive
   outside Earth's atmosphere

This band has an exclamation point at the end of their name
in order to trick you into being excited about ska music.

Number of Apologies Issued to Ms. Jackson

	APOLOGIES
1,000,000,000,000	
7,500,000,000	
5,000,000,000	
2,500,000,000	
0	

Source: OutKast

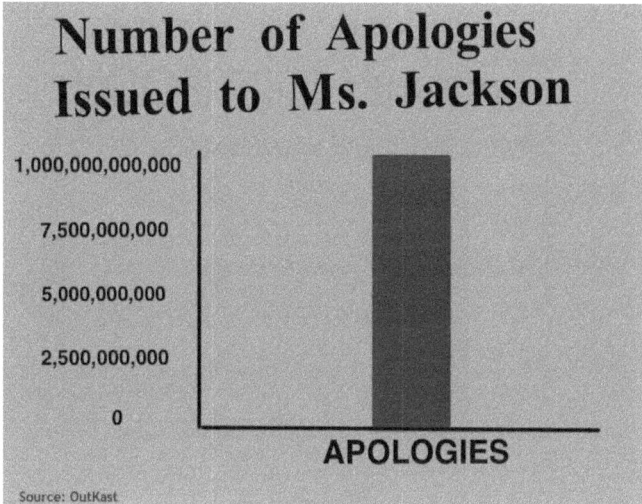

If you look closely, you'll notice that the y-axis of this graph jumps from seven billion to one trillion too quickly.

I never meant to make a faulty Y.
I apologize, the flub was mine.
I'm sorry this graph's bad.
I am for real.

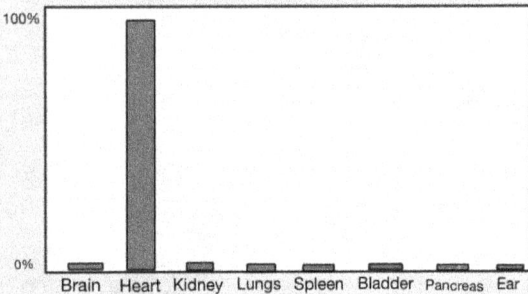

LOCATION OF GROOVE WITHIN THE BODY

Source: Deee-Lite

This song features a slide whistle, which is the musical instrument that looks the most like a tampon.

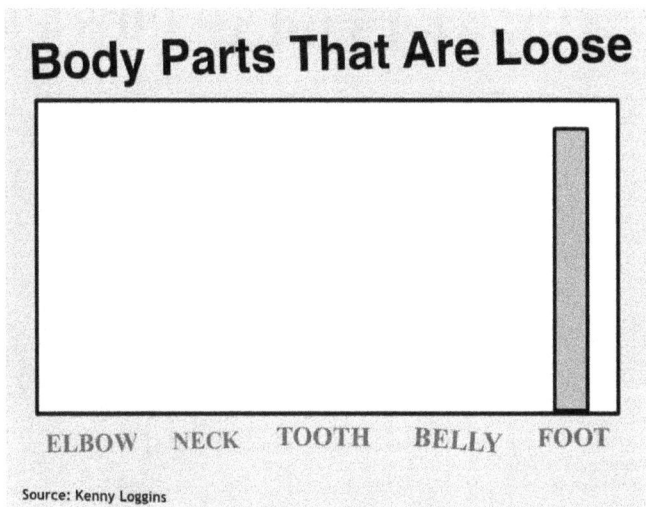

Body Parts That Are Loose

ELBOW   NECK   TOOTH   BELLY   FOOT

Source: Kenny Loggins

The movie *Footloose* is an allegory about Prohibition, which is why Kevin Bacon's character is named Al Capone and carries a Tommy Gun.

Whose Land Is This?

Source: Woody Guthrie

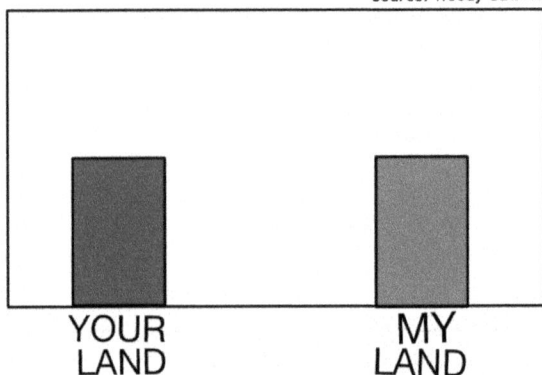

Woody Guthrie was a folk singer who traveled across the country with nothing but a guitar, his songs, a suitcase, a change of clothes, his family (sometimes), money to buy things, identification, extra guitar strings in case some broke, a car or truck, a coat, shoes, socks, underwear, socks, legal documents, toiletries, handkerchiefs, an assistant, his manager, a lawyer, snacks, and his dreams.

Where I Saw Her Standing

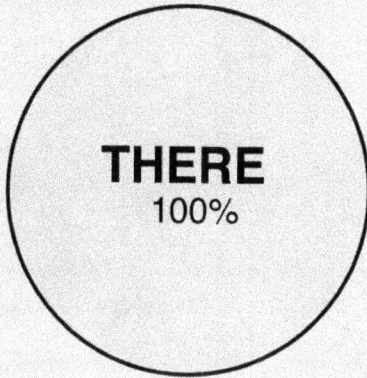

THERE
100%

Source: The Beatles

Hopefully she's still standing there next year, when she turns eighteen, creep. Until then, stop staring at her.

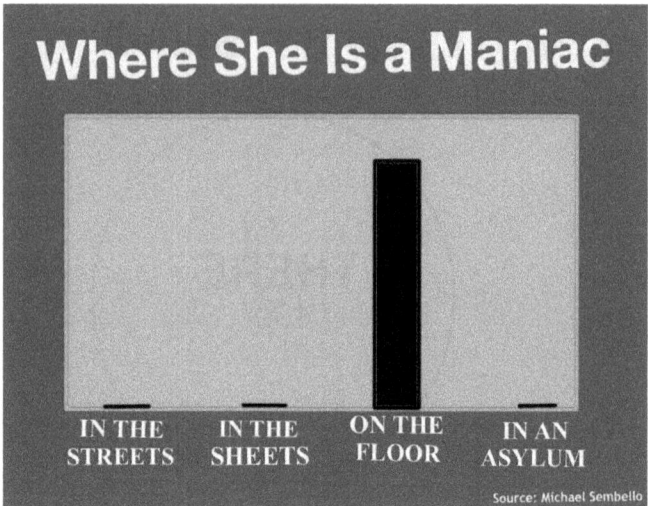

Where She Is a Maniac

| IN THE STREETS | IN THE SHEETS | ON THE FLOOR | IN AN ASYLUM |

Source: Michael Sembello

She's dancing like she's never danced before?
It sounds like she needs more practice dancing.

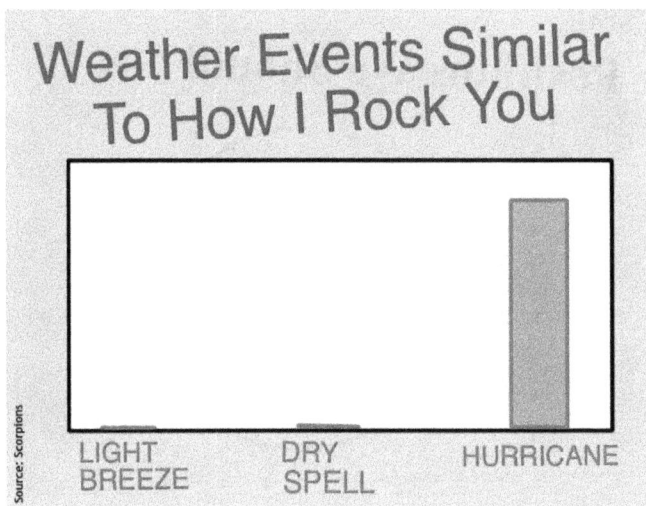

Weather Events Similar To How I Rock You

LIGHT BREEZE — DRY SPELL — HURRICANE

Source: Scorpions

A hurricane is more windy than rocky.

A better sexual metaphor would be "I'm going to make you wet like a hurricane" since tropical cyclones are usually accompanied by thunderstorms and heavy rain.

Positions We Should Get It

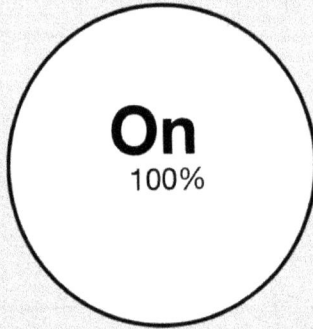

On
100%

Source: Marvin Gaye

At the time he released this song, Marvin Gaye was married to the sister of Motown founder Barry Gordy.

I once wrote a song about having sex with my boss's sister, but it did not go over as well as Marvin Gaye's song.

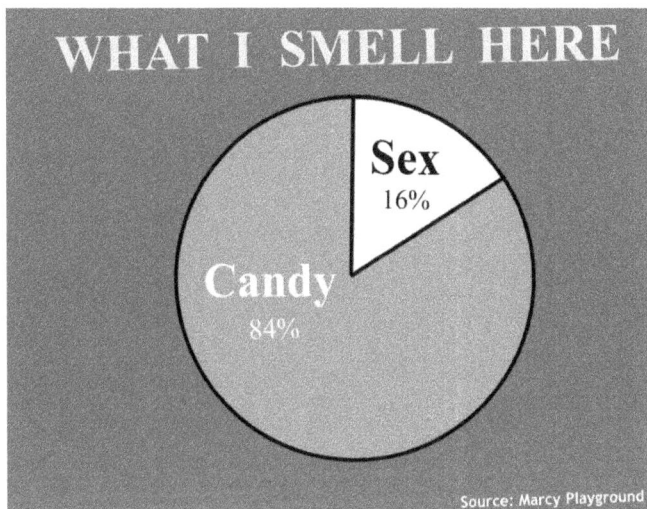

Could you be more specific about what kind of candy you smell?

"This" is probably high-fructose corn syrup.

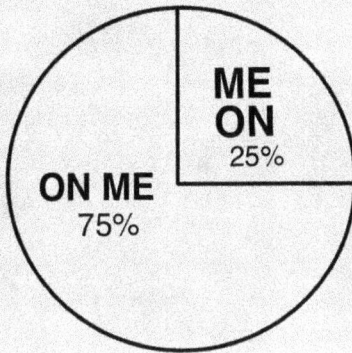

What to Take

ME
ON
25%

ON ME
75%

Source: A-ha

Producing the band A-ha is Norway's second biggest achievement besides awarding the Nobel Peace Prize. Norway's third biggest achievement? Wood.

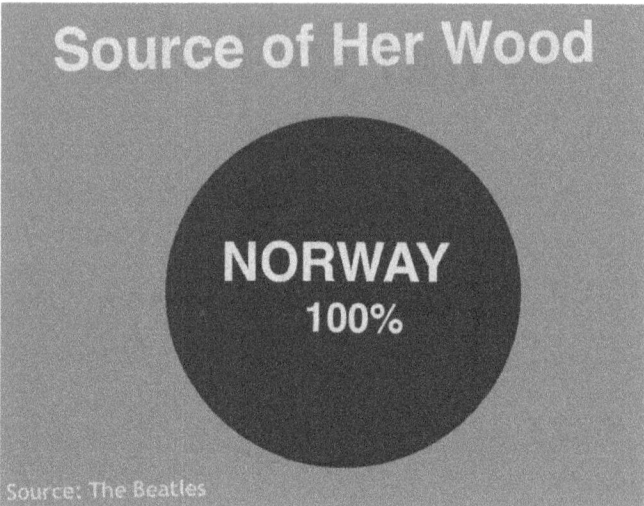

Source of Her Wood

NORWAY
100%

Source: The Beatles

"Norwegian Wood (This Bird Has Flown)" is about a woman who can't afford a chair, but still manages to have sex with one of The Beatles. While she's at work the next day, he sets her apartment on fire.

Who Gives Love a Bad Name

You
100%

Source: Bon Jovi

If your girlfriend shoots you through the heart, you should break up with her (if you survive, which is unlikely).

Relatives with Soul

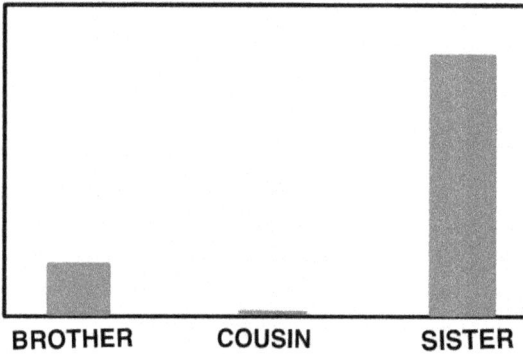

| BROTHER | COUSIN | SISTER |

Sources: Train, Queen

Train's song "Hey, Soul Sister" is based on what its singer imagined the Burning Man festival is like, which is cute, although he is incredibly wrong.

What Weather Phenomena She Is Most Like

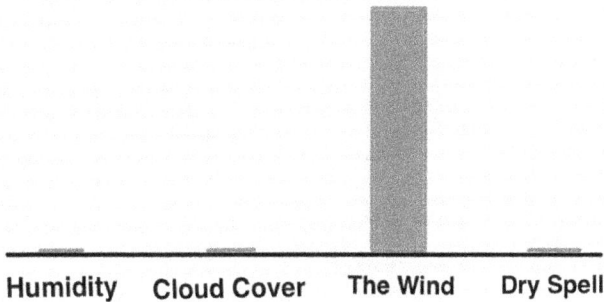

| Humidity | Cloud Cover | The Wind | Dry Spell |

Source: Patrick Swayze

Patrick Swayze sings, acts, and dances in the film *Dirty Dancing*, which makes him a triple threat. He is also a triple threat in *Ghost*, but it's for acting, pottery, and penny lifting, which is less impressive.

Locations of Insane

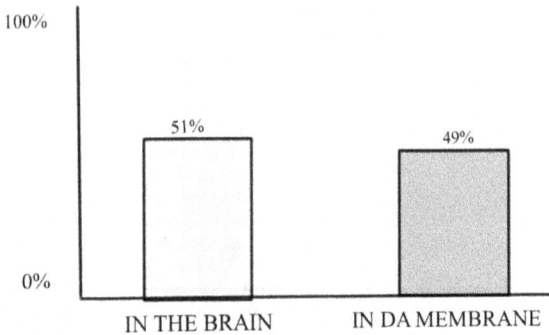

100%

51%

49%

0%

IN THE BRAIN   IN DA MEMBRANE

Source: Cypress Hill

Doctors have yet to find a patient who is insane anywhere other than in the brain.

WHERE TO STAND

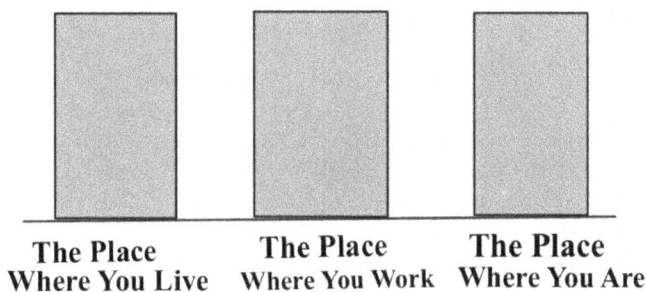

| The Place
Where You Live | The Place
Where You Work | The Place
Where You Are |

Source: R.E.M.

This was R.E.M.'s stupidest song for only two years, from 1989 until 1991, when "Shiny Happy People" was released.

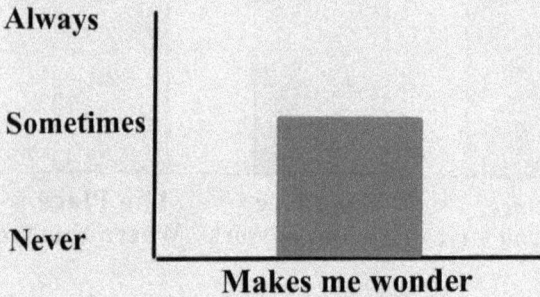

WHEN THE FACT THAT IT'S A JUNGLE MAKES ME WONDER HOW I KEEP FROM GOIN' UNDER

Source: Grandmaster Flash and The Furious Five, feat. Melle Mel & Duke Bootee

"The Message" by Grandmaster Flash and the Furious Five is considered the first rap song with socially conscious lyrics. It was the inspiration for Sir Mix-a-Lot's "Baby Got Back."

WHAT THIS DUDE I SAW LOOKS LIKE

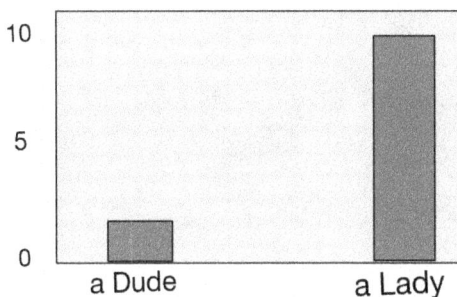

Source: Aerosmith

Half of Aerosmith's songs are about having sex. The other half have yet to be released.

What To Lean On

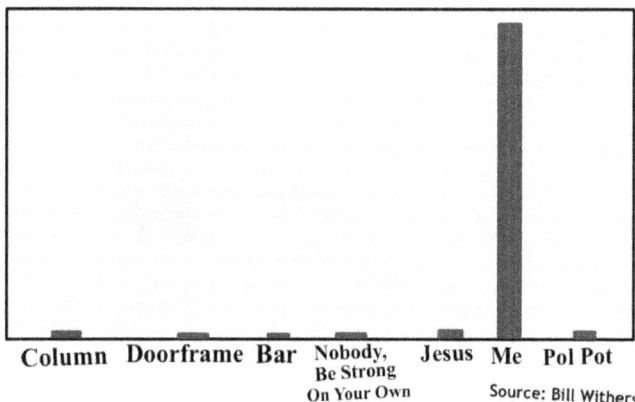

Column	Doorframe	Bar	Nobody, Be Strong On Your Own	Jesus	Me	Pol Pot

Source: Bill Withers

I once tried to lean on Bill Withers, and he wouldn't let me. He said, "Get out of my house, or I'll call the cops. How did you even get in here?" So I think this song is metaphorical rather than literal.

Disposition of Caroline

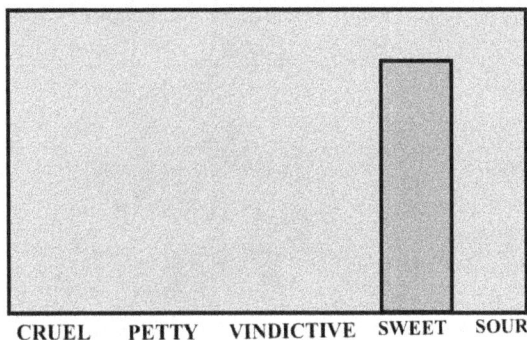

CRUEL   PETTY   VINDICTIVE   SWEET   SOUR

Source: Neil Diamond

This song is about a good-natured girl named Caroline.

Or else it's about a girl named Caroline who has been licked by Neil Diamond.

TYPE OF LOBSTER
THAT WE FOUND

**Rock
Lobster**
100%

Source: The B-52's

The B-52's recorded a version of this song–which is about lobsters–that is almost seven minutes long.

Cost of Falling

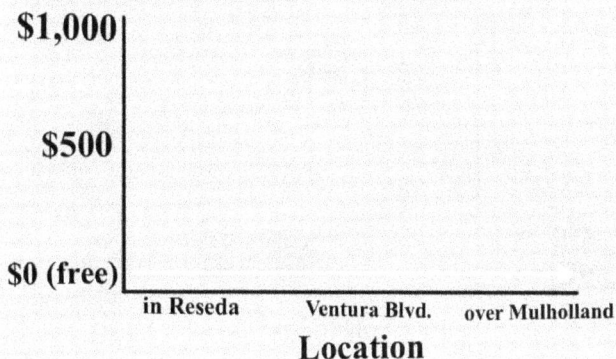

$1,000

$500

$0 (free)

in Reseda   Ventura Blvd.   over Mulholland

Location

Source: Tom Petty

Tom Petty suffered from a disease that made him always look uncomfortable.

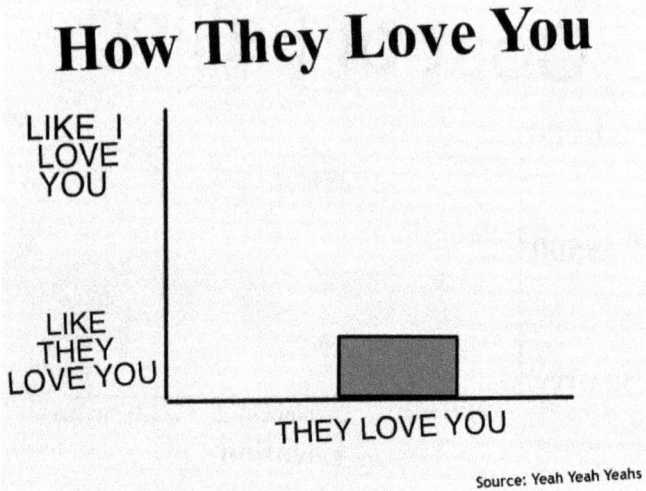

How They Love You

LIKE I
LOVE
YOU

LIKE
THEY
LOVE YOU

THEY LOVE YOU

Source: Yeah Yeah Yeahs

The song "Maps" by Yeah Yeah Yeahs does not offer a thorough discussion of maps.

What I'm Doing with the Devil

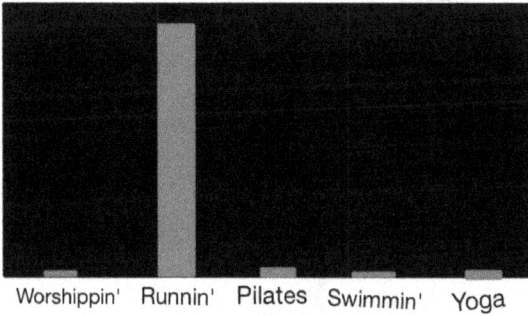

| Worshippin' | Runnin' | Pilates | Swimmin' | Yoga |

Source: Van Halen

Van Helsing, wearing Van Heusen, heard Van Halen.

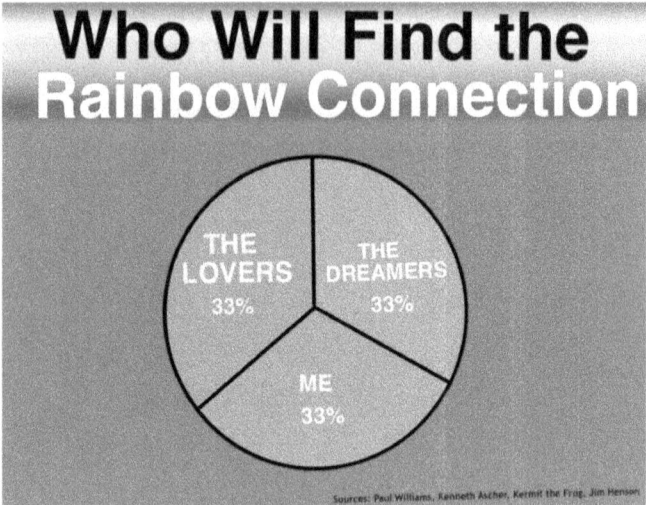

Who Will Find the
Rainbow Connection

THE LOVERS 33%

THE DREAMERS 33%

ME 33%

Sources: Paul Williams, Kenneth Ascher, Kermit the Frog, Jim Henson

It must be difficult if you're a human singer, and you realize this song by a puppet is better than anything you'll ever do.

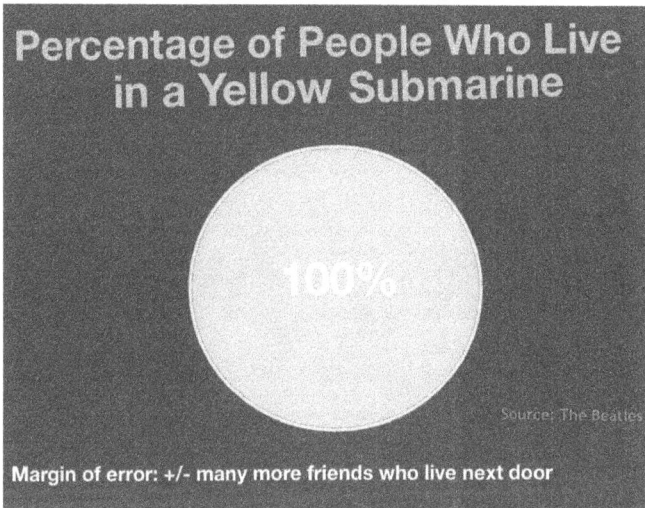

Percentage of People Who Live in a Yellow Submarine

100%

Source: The Beatles

Margin of error: +/- many more friends who live next door

I don't for one second believe that any of The Beatles ever lived in a submarine.

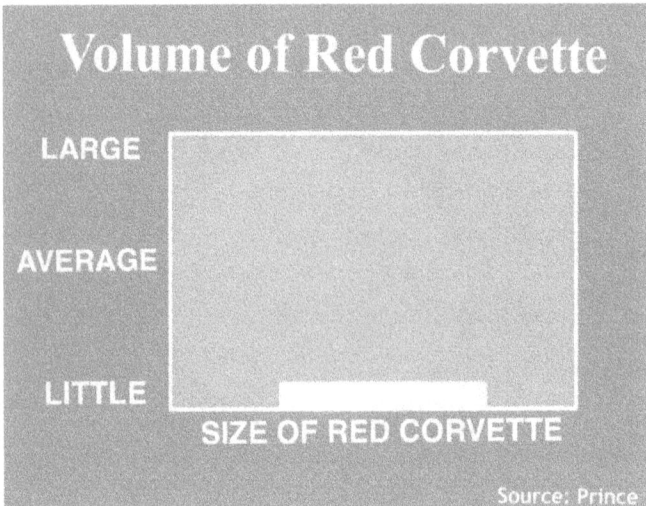

Volume of Red Corvette

LARGE

AVERAGE

LITTLE

SIZE OF RED CORVETTE

Source: Prince

You know your Corvette was too small when a guy who was barely five foot tall complained about how little it was.

What Kind of Time I've Had

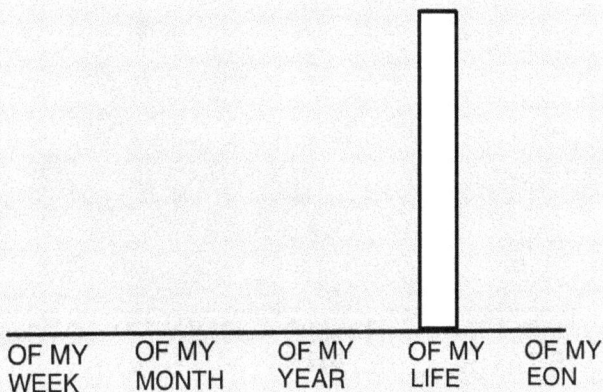

OF MY WEEK	OF MY MONTH	OF MY YEAR	OF MY LIFE	OF MY EON

Source: Frankie Previte, John DeNicola, Donald Markowitz, Bill Medley, and Jennifer Warnes

Once on summer vacation I helped a relative stranger get an abortion. It was *the time of my life*.

What Kind of Stars Break the Mold

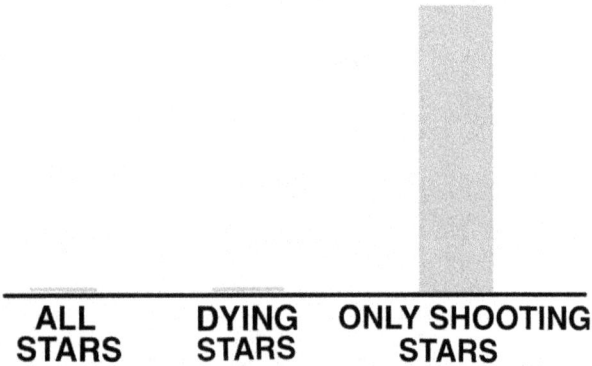

ALL STARS   DYING STARS   ONLY SHOOTING STARS

Source: Smash Mouth

After shooting stars are done breaking the mold, they sometimes have bread thrown at them while performing at small
food festivals.

Appropriate Bodies of Water for Chasing Purposes

1. Rivers
2. Lakes
3. ~~Waterfalls~~

Most bodies of water are stationary, and therefore do not need to be chased.

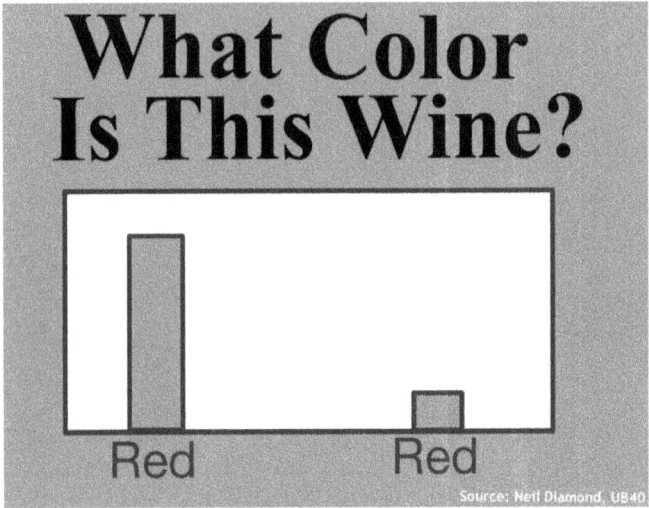

Most red wines are actually purple. So if you want one that looks red, it is good to specify you want a red red wine.

Best Places To Build a Little Birdhouse

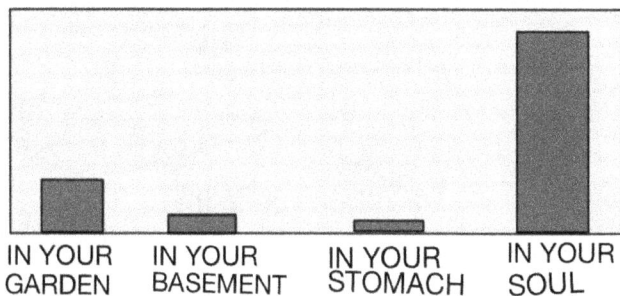

IN YOUR GARDEN   IN YOUR BASEMENT   IN YOUR STOMACH   IN YOUR SOUL

Source: They Might Be Giants

They Might Be Giants were a very popular band at the nerd camp I attended as a child.

Things I'd Do For You

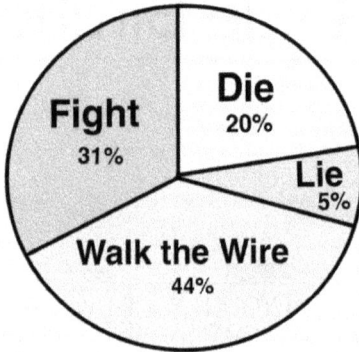

Source: Bryan Adams

Lying is the least romantic thing to do for someone.

Location of Candle

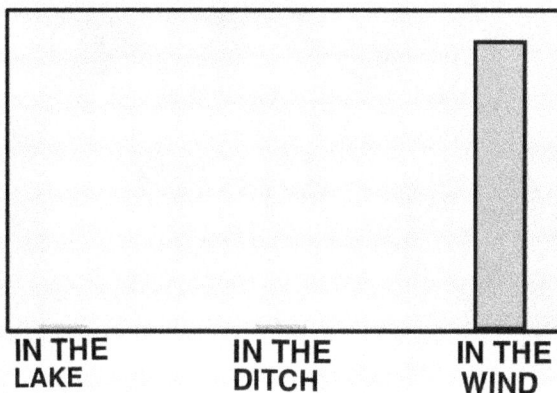

IN THE LAKE	**IN THE DITCH**	**IN THE WIND**

Source: Elton John, Bernie Taupin

The song "Candle in the Wind" was originally about Marilyn Monroe and was later updated as a tribute to Princess Diana. It's pretty clear Elton John has a thing for blonde women.

A fun fact about The Mamas & The Papas is that a daughter of their members formed the group Wilson Phillips with daughters of The Beach Boys' Brian Wilson. A less fun fact is that "Papa" John Phillips was accused of having a 10-year incestuous relationship with another of his daughters.

HOW THINGS ARE GONNA GET

1. O-o-h child, easier
2. O-o-h child, brighter

Source: The Five Stairsteps

"O-o-h Child" is a great song whose title is over punctuated (too many hyphens).

Who This Little Ditty Is About

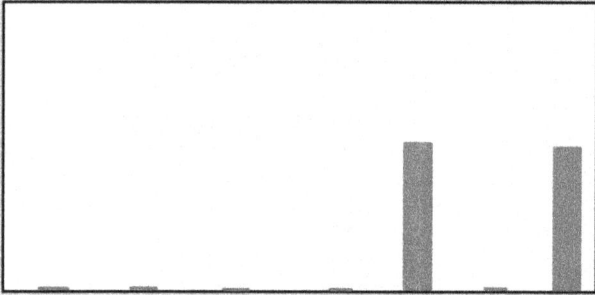

| Peter | Sean | Michelle | Rosa | Jack | Amos | Diane |

Source: John Cougar

It's pretty sexist that Jack gets top billing in the song "Jack and Diane." Alphabetically, Diane's name comes first.

List of Popular Steadies

1. Brenda
2. Eddie

Source: Billy Joel

According to the lyrics to "Scenes from an Italian Restuar-ant," Billy Joel attended a very progressive high school, where Brenda was voted king of the prom and Eddie was elected queen.

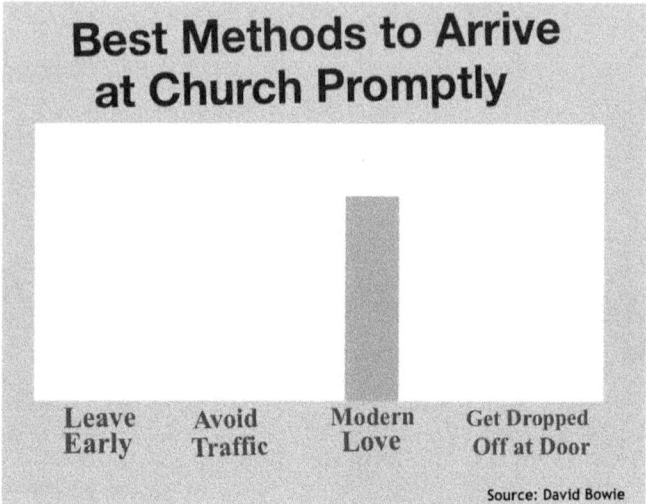

Best Methods to Arrive at Church Promptly

| Leave Early | Avoid Traffic | Modern Love | Get Dropped Off at Door |

Source: David Bowie

Say what you will about David Bowie, but he was always prompt for religious services.

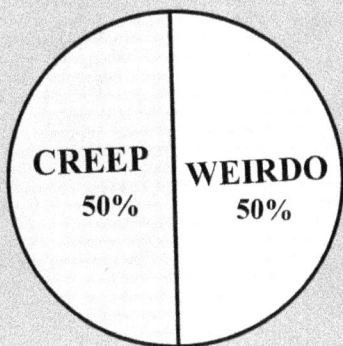

Reasons I Don't Belong Here

CREEP 50%

WEIRDO 50%

Source: Radiohead

Most creeps are weirdos, but not all weirdos are creeps.

Things We Don't Need

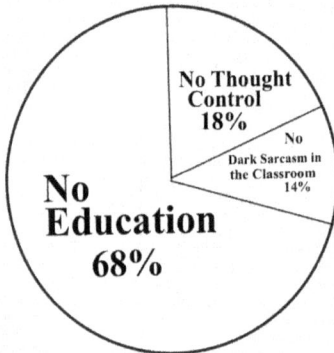

No Thought
Control
18%

No
Dark Sarcasm in
the Classroom
14%

No
Education
68%

Source: Pink Floyd

Pink Floyd is currently considered one of the best Pink Floyd cover bands around.

HOW FAR I WOULD WALK JUST TO BE THE MAN WHO FALLS DOWN AT YOUR DOOR

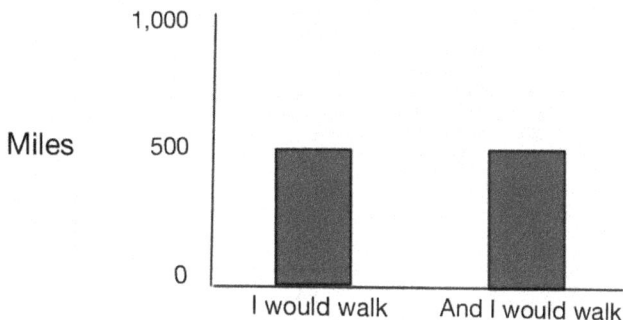

Source: The Proclaimers

Members of the Scottish duo The Proclaimers first met when they were competing with each other in an Elvis Costello lookalike contest.

BODY PARTS THAT WILL GO ON

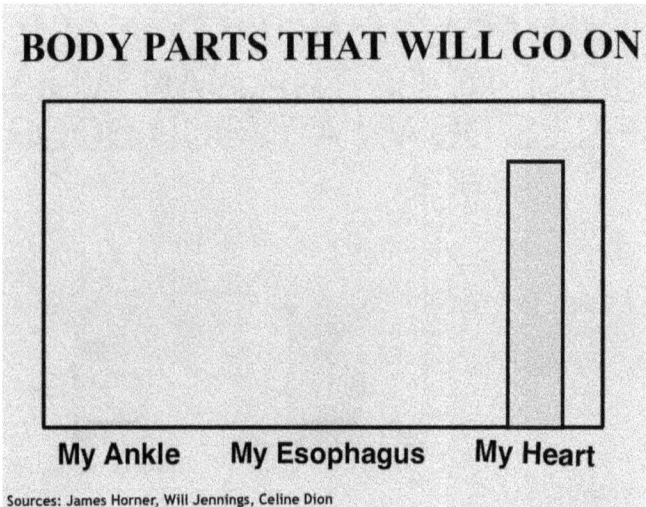

My Ankle   My Esophagus   My Heart

Sources: James Horner, Will Jennings, Celine Dion

Did you know?

Celine Dion recorded the theme song for the film *Titanic* while submerged under water.

Rights You Need To Fight For

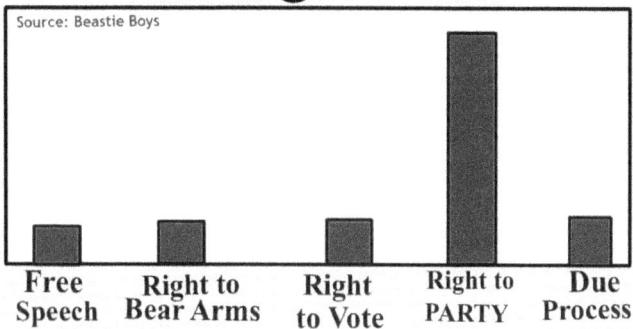

Source: Beastie Boys

| Free Speech | Right to Bear Arms | Right to Vote | Right to PARTY | Due Process |

According to the ACLU, the "right to party" is not guaranteed by the Constitution. At least, that's what they told me when I called them from jail after I was arrested for partying my neighbor to death.

Current Whereabouts of the Hotstepper

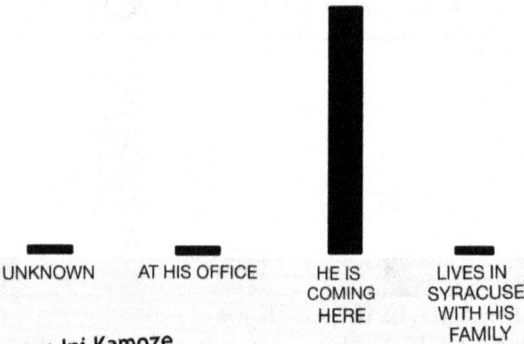

| UNKNOWN | AT HIS OFFICE | HE IS COMING HERE | LIVES IN SYRACUSE WITH HIS FAMILY |

Source: Ini Kamoze

Hotsteppers are seldom welcome in houses with floors made of ice.

Type of Horse I Rode

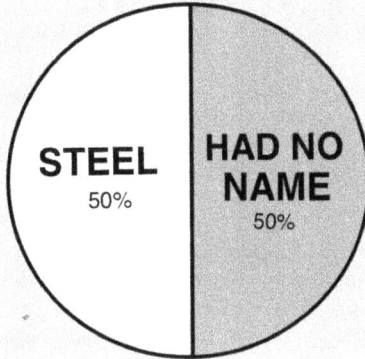

STEEL
50%

HAD NO NAME
50%

Sources: Bon Jovi, America

Many people mistakenly believe "A Horse with No Name" is by Neil Young because the singer sounds so cantankerous and weary.

What Kind of
Virgin I'm Like

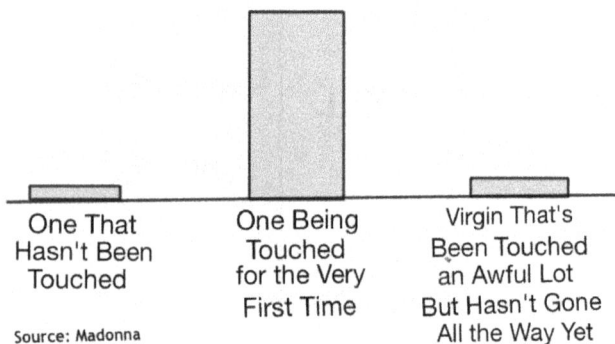

| One That Hasn't Been Touched | One Being Touched for the Very First Time | Virgin That's Been Touched an Awful Lot But Hasn't Gone All the Way Yet |

Source: Madonna

Virgins are frequently not skilled at sexual intercourse, so making somebody feel like a virgin during sex is not necessarily good.

What I'm Doing, on a Jet Plane

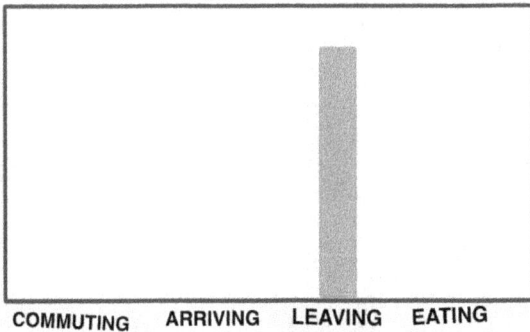

COMMUTING   ARRIVING   LEAVING   EATING

Source: John Denver

If you were leaving on a propellor-powered aircraft, I might try to stop you, but if it's a jet plane, no way.

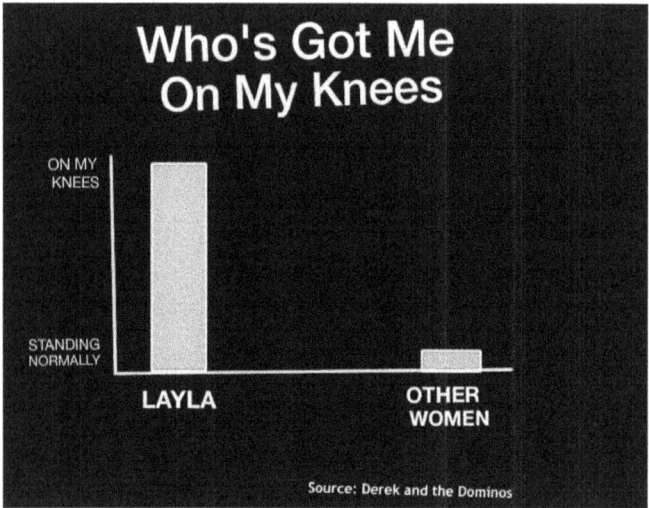

The woman who inspired Eric Clapton to write "Layla" also inspired George Harrison to write The Beatles' classic "Something." She later married a property developer.

Reasons to Go Uptown

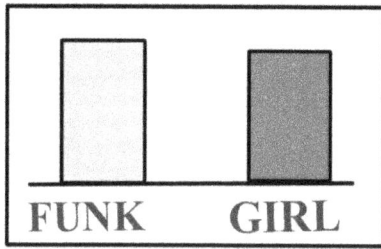

Sources: Billy Joel, Mark Ronson feat. Bruno Mars

It is surprising that Billy Joel was able to successfully court a woman from uptown, since he is synonymous with the gritty, hardcore inner city.

Kind of Day It's Been Without You, My Friend

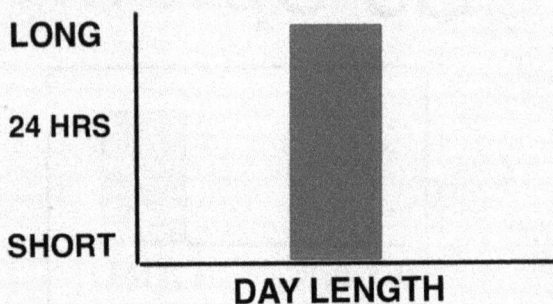

LONG

24 HRS

SHORT

DAY LENGTH

You should never break up with someone the day we set our clocks back an hour.

Popular Ways to Party

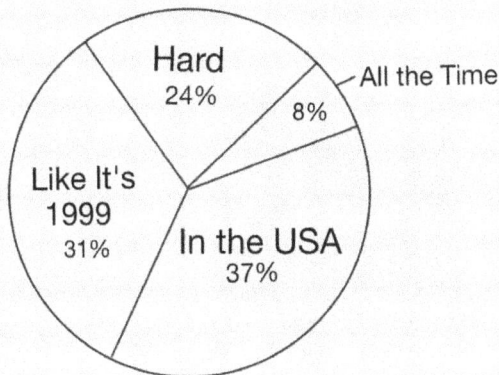

Hard
24%

All the Time
8%

Like It's
1999
31%

In the USA
37%

Sources: Andrew W.K., Prince, Eddie Murphy, and Miley Cyrus

If you host a party, and your boyfriend leaves at the same time as your friend, while holding her hand, it is acceptable to cry.

What Will Be Televised

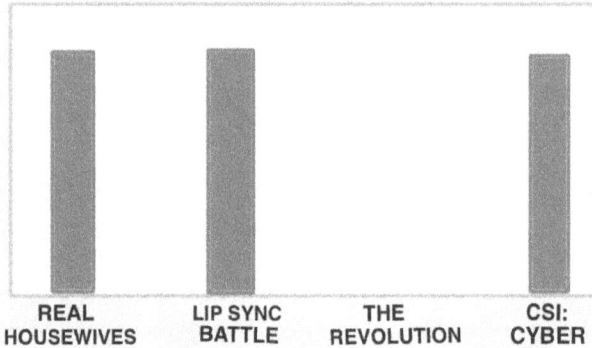

| REAL HOUSEWIVES | LIP SYNC BATTLE | THE REVOLUTION | CSI: CYBER |

Source: Gil Scott-Heron

The French and Industrial Revolutions were not televised (because television had not been invented yet).

Did you know?

Every member of the band Queen had the last name Mercury except for John Deacon, Brian May, and Roger Taylor.

Number of Bads Needed To Describe Leroy Brown

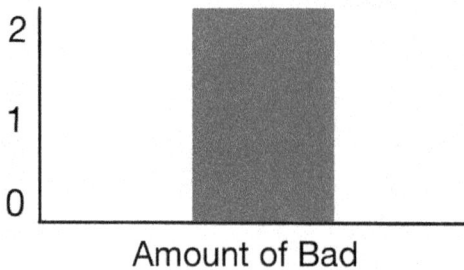

Amount of Bad

Source: Jim Croce

Before he became a songwriter, Jim Croce was one of America's finest bar fight historians.

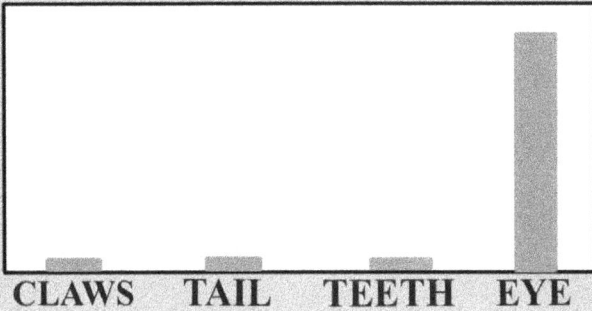

Important Parts of a Tiger's Anatomy

CLAWS   TAIL   TEETH   EYE

Source: Survivor

Although it doesn't sound as ferocious, "Eye of the Rabbit" would actually be a better vision to attain.

Women In Possession of a Big Ol' Butt

1. Tanya
2. Shirley
3. Irene
4. Theresa

5. Sonya
6. Melissa
7. Little Keisha

Note: Tina, Brenda, and Lisa omitted from study because it did not focus on big ole butts

Source: E.U. (Experience Unlimited)

If Bryan Adams told me he liked big butts, I might suspect he was lying to protect someone.

What I Said When They Tried To Make Me Go To Rehab

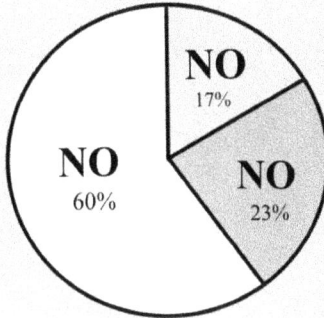

NO
17%

NO
60%

NO
23%

Source: Amy Winehouse

Like millions of adults, Amy Winehouse once recorded a duet with Tony Bennett.

How You Feel About Startin' Somethin'

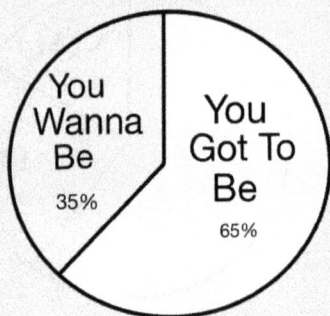

You Wanna Be 35%

You Got To Be 65%

Source: Michael Jackson

If you are startin' somethin', you should start with the man in the mirror.

How Often I've Got Nothing But Love, Babe

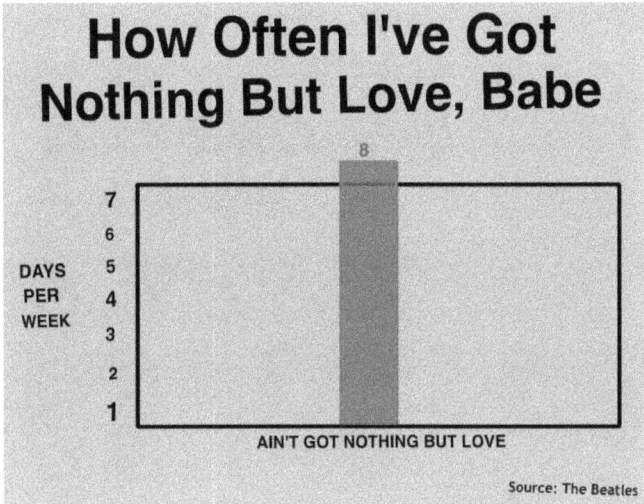

DAYS PER WEEK

8

7
6
5
4
3
2
1

AIN'T GOT NOTHING BUT LOVE

Source: The Beatles

In the United Kingdom, weeks have eight days, and there are 45 weeks in a year.

69

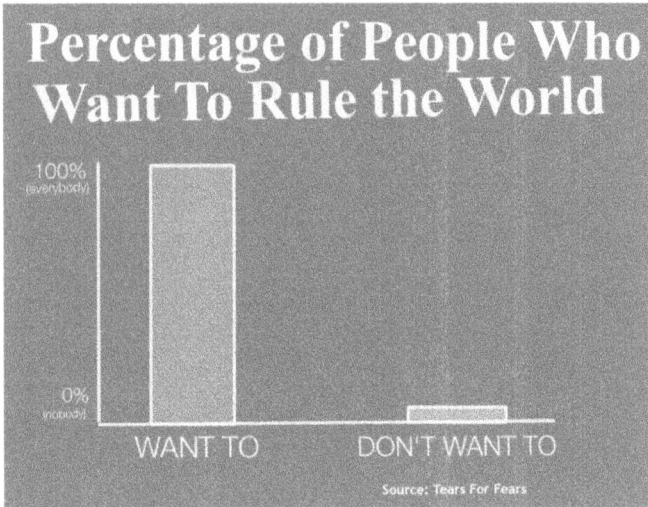

Percentage of People Who Want To Rule the World

100% (everybody)

0% (nobody)

WANT TO   DON'T WANT TO

Source: Tears For Fears

In a true democracy, everybody *does* rule the world.

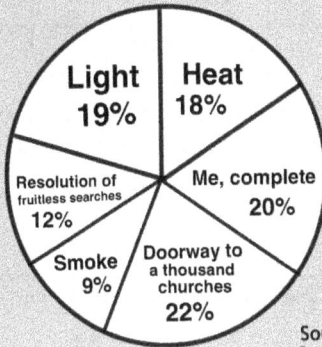

Substances Found In Your Eyes

Light 19%

Heat 18%

Resolution of fruitless searches 12%

Me, complete 20%

Smoke 9%

Doorway to a thousand churches 22%

Sources:
Peter Gabriel; Jerome Kern; et al

If you are over 65, you should have your eyes checked for glaucoma every one to two years.

What I Wish You'd Do
In Relation to That Ledge

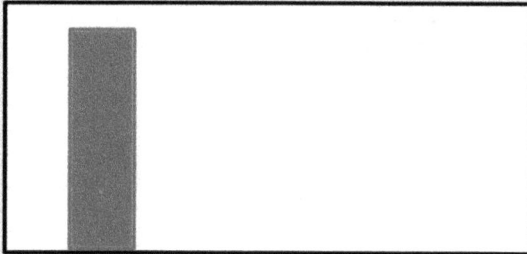

STEP BACK FROM	JUMP OFF OF

Source: Third Eye Blind

One of the leading causes of suicide in America is listening to too much Third Eye Blind.

REASONS WE'RE UP ALL NIGHT

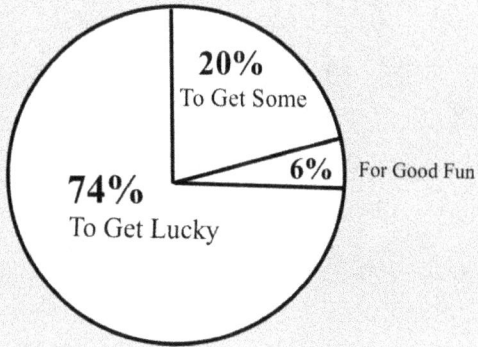

20%
To Get Some

6% For Good Fun

74%
To Get Lucky

Source: Daft Punk (research assistance by Pharrell Williams)

Getting lucky, *getting some*, and *having good fun* are all synonyms for heavy petting.

Optimal Times to Light My Fire

RIGHT NOW
TIME WHEN, IF WE TRY
WE CAN ONLY LOSE AND
OUR LOVE BECOMES
A FUNERAL PYRE
TIME TO WALLOW IN MIRE
TIME TO HESITATE
POOR
DECENT
GOOD
THE ENTIRE
NIGHT IS
ON FIRE!
Quality of Fire

Source: The Doors

The lyrics of Doors singer Jim Morrison are often considered poetry by people who have never read any actual poems.

What She Told Me To Do This Way

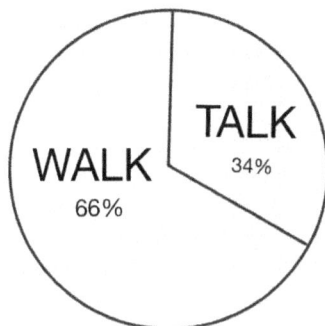

TALK
34%

WALK
66%

Source: Aerosmith

If Aerosmith was an actor, it would be Charlie Sheen.

Percentage of People
Who Were Kung Fu Fighting

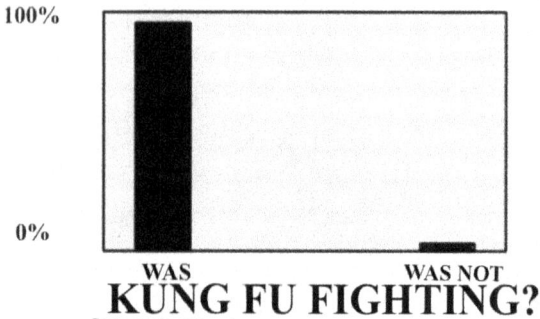

100%

0%

WAS   WAS NOT
KUNG FU FIGHTING?
Source: Carl Douglas

You must be mistaken, for I have never kung fu fought.

Size of Dancer

Huge	
Regular	
Tiny	

Dancer

Source: Elton John

The tiny dancer cried tiny tears when she first heard this song, for she had always been told she was a normal sized dancer.

Subjects I Don't Know Much About

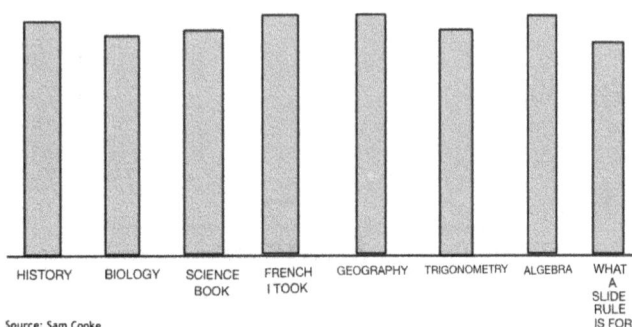

| HISTORY | BIOLOGY | SCIENCE BOOK | FRENCH I TOOK | GEOGRAPHY | TRIGONOMETRY | ALGEBRA | WHAT A SLIDE RULE IS FOR |

Source: Sam Cooke

Another thing Sam Cooke doesn't know much about is how to find words that rhyme with algebra.

Wildness by Geographical Direction

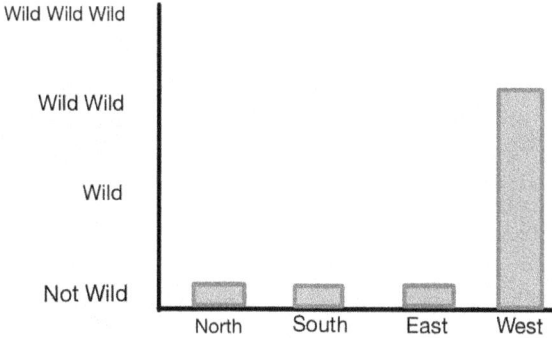

Source: The Escape Club, Will Smith

"Deadwood" is considered a great TV show, but they really missed an opportunity to use Will Smith's "Wild, Wild West" song on the soundtrack.

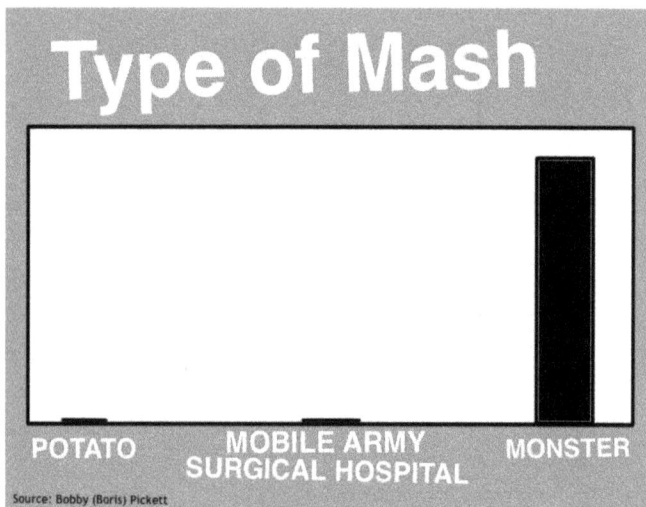

Type of Mash

POTATO   MOBILE ARMY SURGICAL HOSPITAL   MONSTER

Source: Bobby (Boris) Pickett

If you're a songwriter looking to get a foot in the door, the Halloween novelty song field is not terribly crowded.

Amount Shook Up

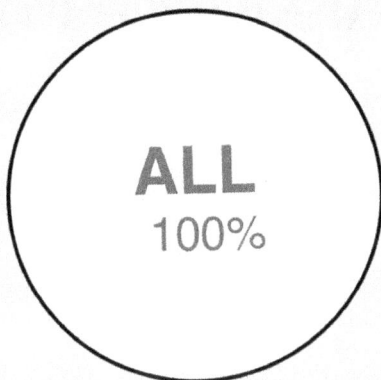

ALL
100%

Sources: Elvis Presley, Otis Blackwell

Elvis Presley portrayed a prisoner in *Jailhouse Rock* and later drew on that experience to portray a prisoner of fame at the end of his life.

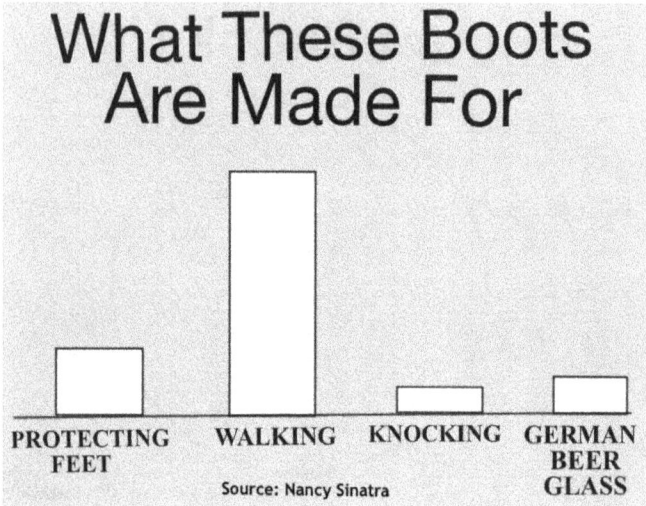

What These Boots Are Made For

| PROTECTING FEET | WALKING | KNOCKING | GERMAN BEER GLASS |

Source: Nancy Sinatra

"Can I walk in these boots?"
"Yes, I made them for that purpose."

What Was Jeremiah?

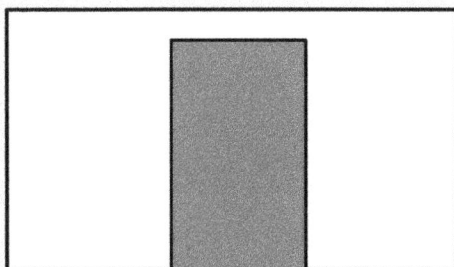

BULLFROG

Source: Three Dog Night

The original lyrics stated that "Jeremiah was a prophet," which makes a lot more sense.

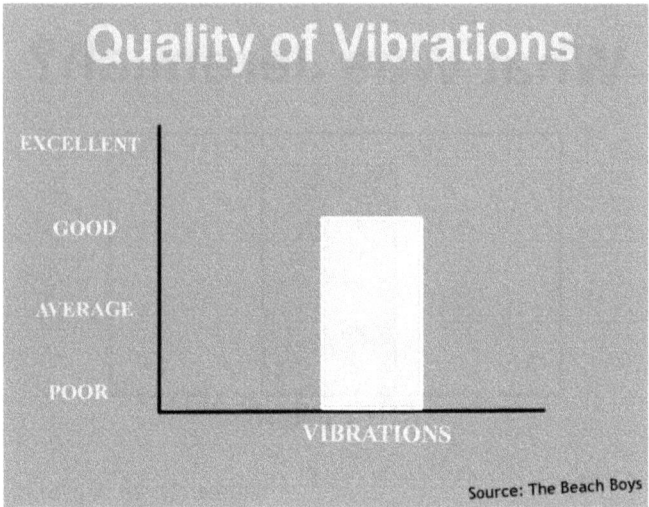

Good vibrations might be signs of an earthquake. Visit https://www.fema.gov/emergency-managers/risk-management/earthquake for more information.

Who Is on Fire?

I'M 50%

THAT GIRL 50%

Sources: Bruce Springsteen, Alicia Keys

If you see someone on fire, you should always call 911 before writing a song.

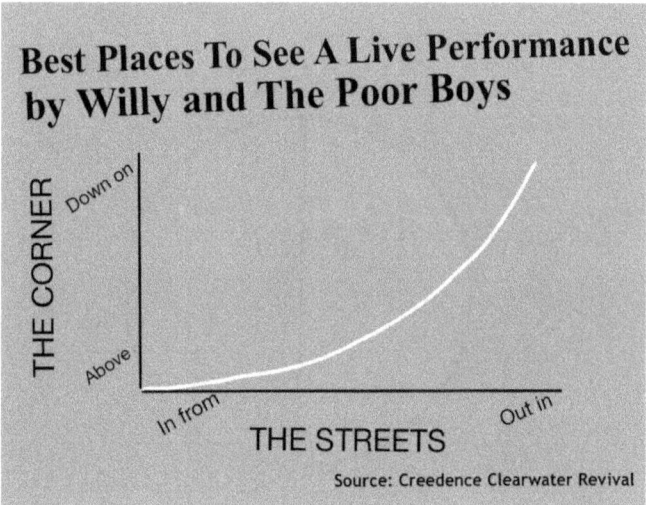

Best Places To See A Live Performance by Willy and The Poor Boys

THE CORNER / THE STREETS — Down on / Above / In from / Out in

Source: Creedence Clearwater Revival

"Where's your next gig, Willy?"

"On the corner."

"Good luck with that."

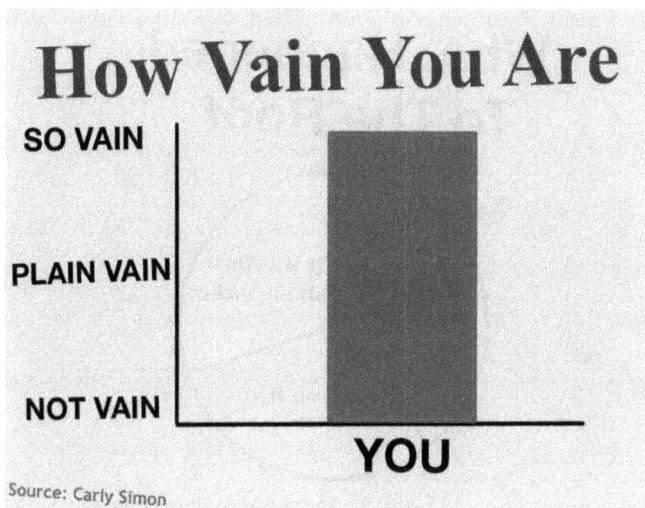

How Vain You Are

SO VAIN

PLAIN VAIN

NOT VAIN

YOU

Source: Carly Simon

If you think a guy is too vain, writing a hit song about him isn't really going to help the situation.

What Happened To The Roof

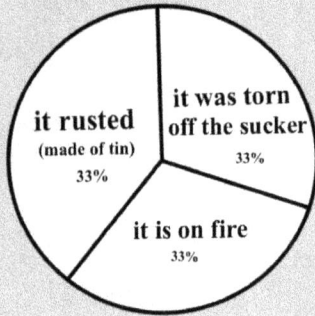

it rusted
(made of tin)
33%

it was torn off the sucker
33%

it is on fire
33%

Source: The B-52's, Parliament, Rock Master Scott & the Dynamic Three

Homeowners should have their roof inspected by a licensed expert every two years.

People Who Could Reach Me

Source: Dusty Springfield

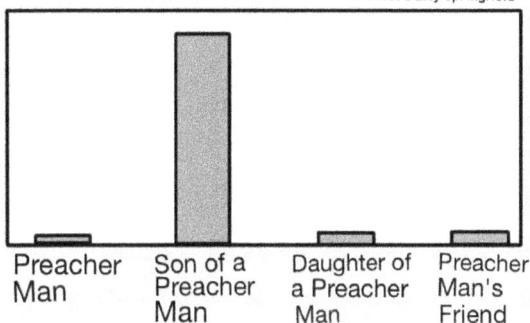

| Preacher Man | Son of a Preacher Man | Daughter of a Preacher Man | Preacher Man's Friend |

"Our daughter sure gets excited whenever the preacher comes to visit. Maybe she'll grow up to be a nun! Or else she is having sex with the preacher's son."

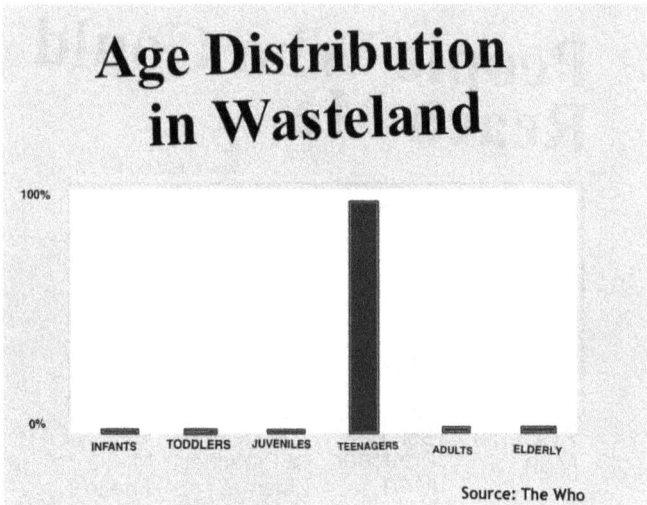

"Pete, should we call this song 'Teenage Wasteland'?"
"No, Roger. I think 'Baba O'Riley' is a better title."

When You Look Wonderful

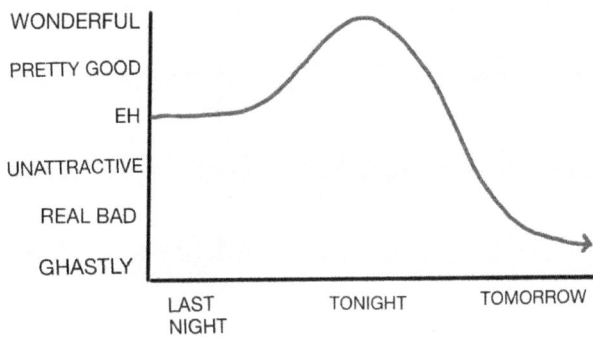

Source: Eric Clapton

This song is about the same woman described in "Layla" and "Something" by The Beatles. Not too shabby.

Who Ground Control Is Trying To Contact

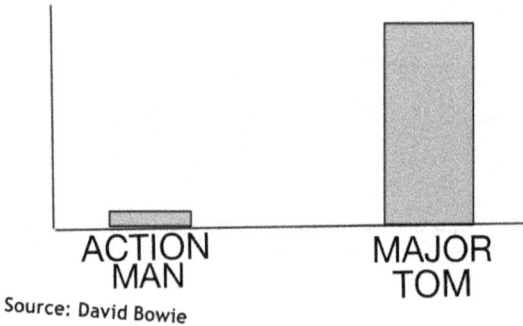

ACTION
MAN

MAJOR
TOM

Source: David Bowie

Major Tom survives by eating "protein pills," which is astronaut slang for globs of semen floating in zero gravity.

What He Drinks Before He Sings

WHISKEY DRINK 25%   VODKA DRINK 25%

LAGER DRINK 25%   CIDER DRINK 25%

Source: Chumbawamba

This tub, the Inspector noted, *has truly been thumped*.

THINGS I'VE SEEN

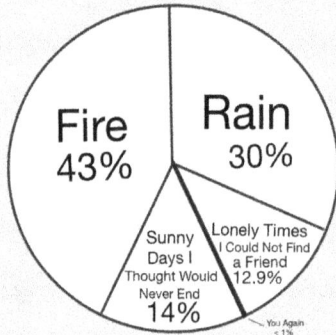

Fire 43%

Rain 30%

Sunny Days I Thought Would Never End 14%

Lonely Times I Could Not Find a Friend 12.9%

You Again < 1%

Source: James Taylor

Did you know?

Before they started selling coffee, Starbucks was a chain of James Taylor CD stores.

Duran Duran is comprised of seven keyboard players.

What London Is Doing?

Source: The Clash

It has been pointed out that London is also drowning, but that is only a concern if you live by the river.

If you weren't always asleep during prime go-go hours, this wouldn't be a problem.

Ratio of Turntables to Microphones

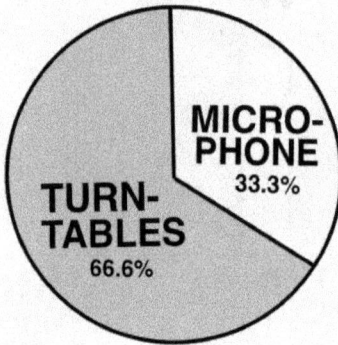

MICRO-PHONE 33.3%

TURN-TABLES 66.6%

Source: Beck

I was sad that I only had two turntables and a microphone, until I met a man who had no turntables and a microphone.

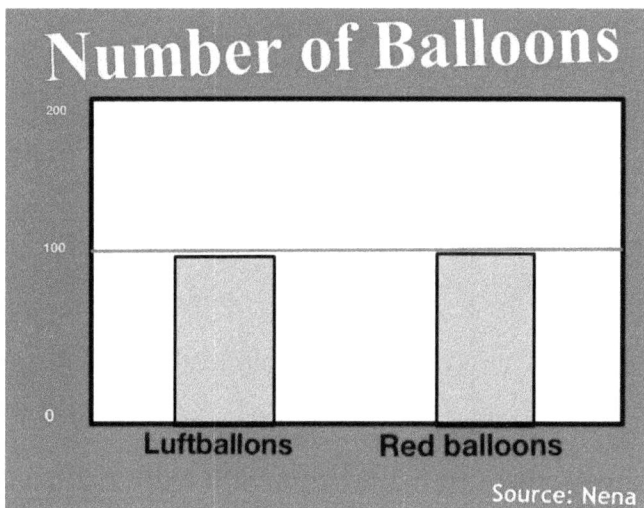

This is a politically charged song about the dangers of having too many balloons.

Emotional States of Jealous Guy

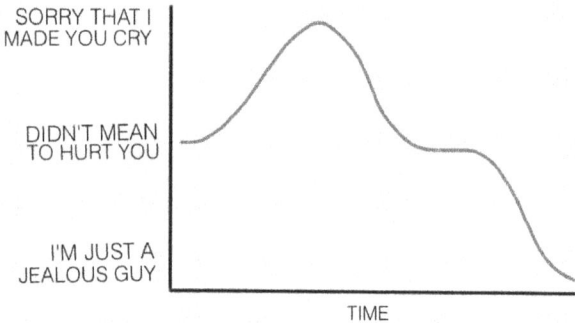

SORRY THAT I MADE YOU CRY

DIDN'T MEAN TO HURT YOU

I'M JUST A JEALOUS GUY

TIME

Source: John Lennon

This is a lovely song that may be about apologizing for domestic violence.

How Much I Miss You

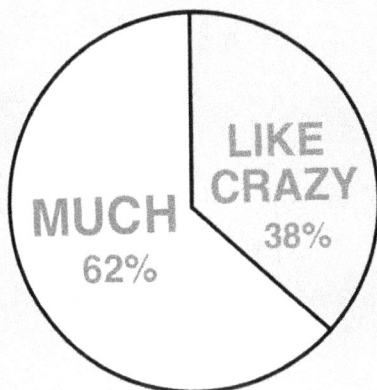

LIKE CRAZY 38%

MUCH 62%

Source: Janet Jackson, Natalie Cole

You know who's not missing you? John Waite.
Not at all.

PERCENTAGE ALONG THE WATCHTOWER

ALL
100%

Sources: Bob Dylan, Jimi Hendrix

Jimi Hendrix didn't write this song, but he should still get credit for it.

Who To Call If There's Something Strange In Your Neighborhood

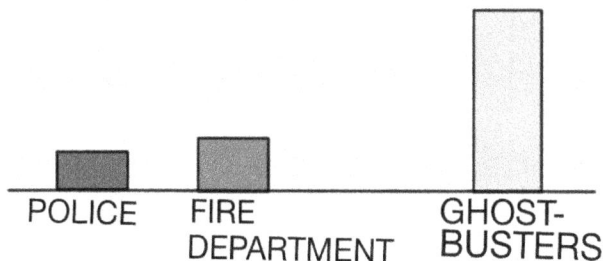

POLICE   FIRE   GHOST-
          DEPARTMENT   BUSTERS

Source: Ray Parker, Jr.

Police would seem cooler if they called themselves *Crookbusters*. Same with firemen and *Smokebusters*.

Mental State During Apocalyptic Events

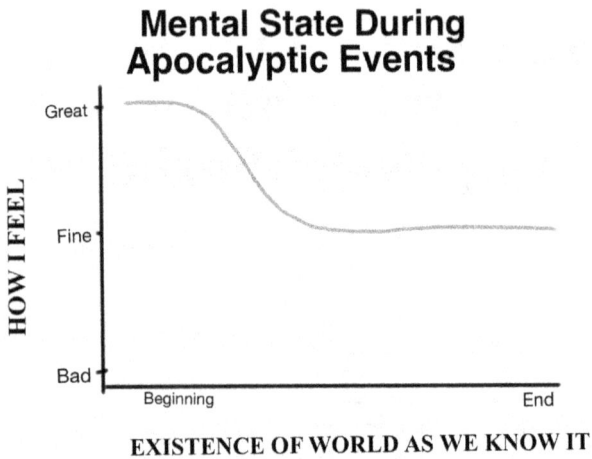

EXISTENCE OF WORLD AS WE KNOW IT

Source: R.E.M.

Leonard Bernstein.

WHEN WE ARE YOUNG

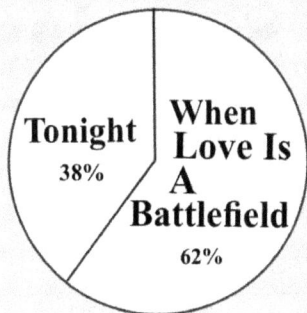

Tonight 38%	When Love Is A Battlefield 62%

Source: fun., Pat Benatar

I once had a next-door neighbor whose name was Young. He must be in his 40s by now.

When I Wear My Sunglasses

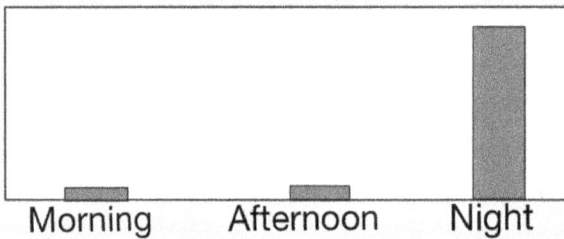

Morning   Afternoon   Night

Source: Corey Hart

The original title for this song was "I Don't Understand What Sunglasses Are For."

Color Palette of My Dreams

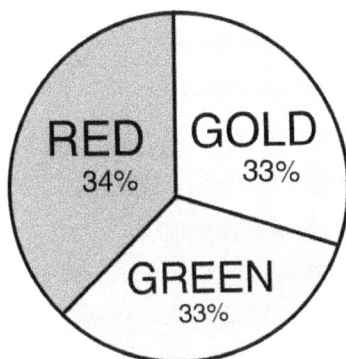

RED
34%

GOLD
33%

GREEN
33%

Source: Culture Club

That doesn't seem like how palette should be spelled, but it's what the dictionary said.

WHO WE SALUTE

Those About
To Rock
100%

Source: AC/DC

Each year we honor the veterans of Rock N Roll by saluting them during Rocktober.

THINGS WE CAN DO TOMORROW

1. Drive around this town
2. Let the cops chase us around
3. Find something that might take the place of the past, which is gone
4. Address jealousy as if it was a person

Source: Gin Blossoms

"911, what's your emergency?"

"I think my neighbor is hitting his wife."

"We can't send anyone, all our squad cars are busy chasing around some local teenagers."

"Well, send someone as soon as you can, he's a real jealous guy."

What Kind of Trip It's Been

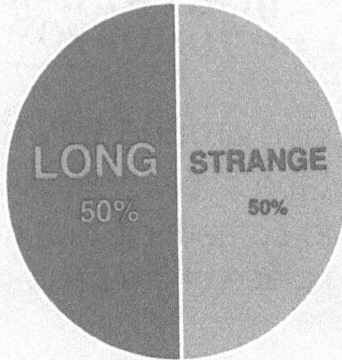

LONG 50% | STRANGE 50%

Source: The Grateful Dead

The Grateful Dead were known for their psychedelic "space jams" which inspired the Michael Jordan film.

Amount of Legit and Quit

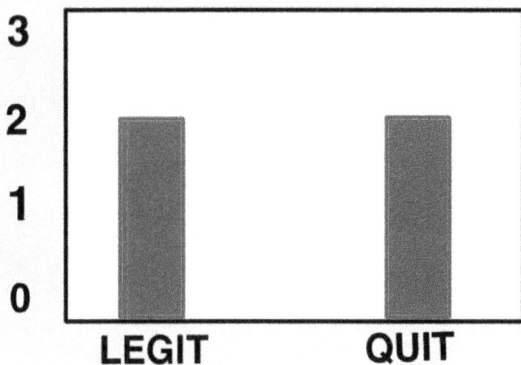

3

2

1

0

LEGIT   QUIT

Source: Hammer

If all you have is a hammer, everything looks like a nail, or a debt collection notice.

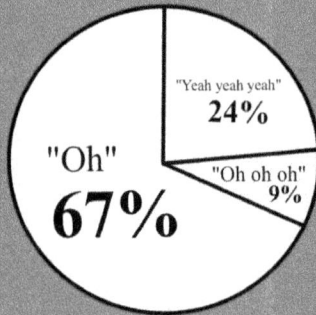

How We Think the Best Song Ever Went

"Yeah yeah yeah" 24%

"Oh oh oh" 9%

"Oh" 67%

Source: One Direction

I just made this one in a desperate attempt to seem relevant to the kids of today.

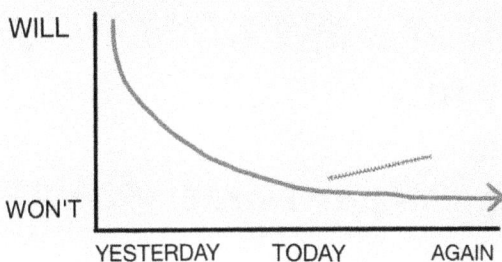

Statistical probability of getting fooled again

WILL

WON'T

YESTERDAY   TODAY   AGAIN

Source: The Who

Did you know?

Before they started writing CSI theme songs, The Who was a successful British rock band.

Things That Were Yellow

1. The stars
2. Title of song I wrote
3. My turn
4. You
5. Color of line I drew

Source: Coldplay

This is one of the most successful songs ever written about a bunch of things that are yellow.

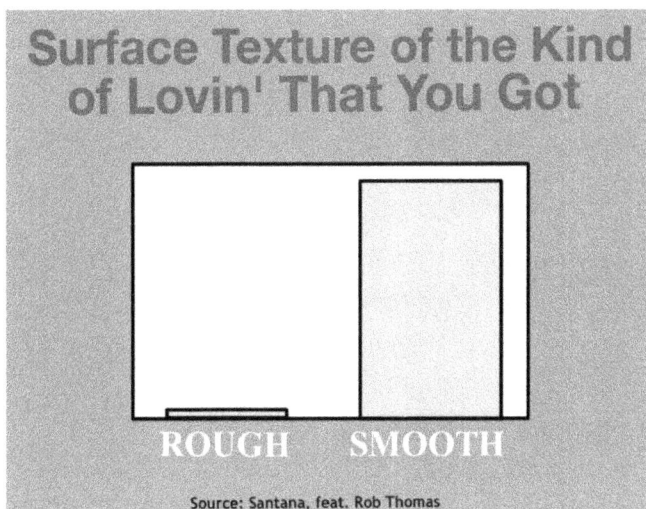

Surface Texture of the Kind of Lovin' That You Got

ROUGH   SMOOTH

Source: Santana, feat. Rob Thomas

This song is a collaboration between music legend Carlos Santana and the guy who sang "Smooth" with Carlos Santana.

You're Gonna Have To Face That You're Addicted To

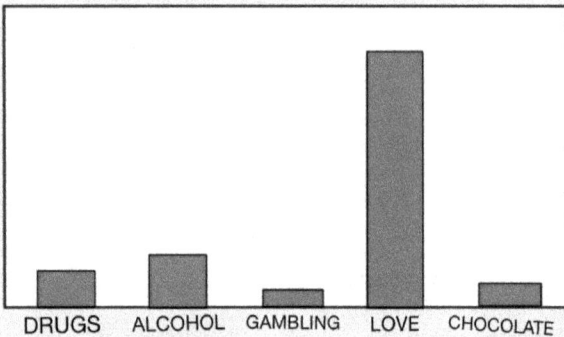

DRUGS   ALCOHOL   GAMBLING   LOVE   CHOCOLATE

Source: Robert Palmer

Robert Palmer focused on the ailment of love in his hit songs "Addicted to Love" and "Bad Case of Loving You (Doctor, Doctor)." But even more dangerous than love is heart disease, which is what killed him.

"Fuck tha Police" is a song about rapper Ice Cube's desire to have sex with police officers.

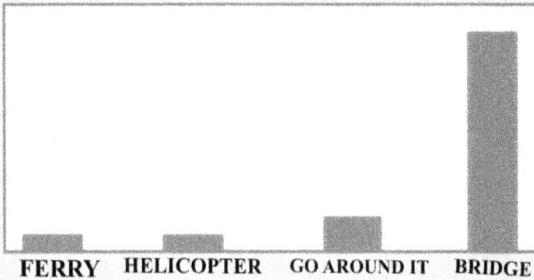

Best Method For Crossing Body of Troubled Waters

FERRY   HELICOPTER   GO AROUND IT   BRIDGE

Source: Simon and Garfunkel

Sure, thanks for the bridge. But those waters will still be troubled tomorrow, so you're not really offering a solution.

Things Mama Said To Me

Knock You Out 31%

Told Me Not To Come 28%

"You Better Shop Around" 18%

"When You Gonna Live Your Life Right?" 23%

Sources: LL Cool J, Three Dog Night & Randy Newman, Cyndi Lauper, Smokey Robinson and The Miracles

Did you know?

LL Cool J is an abbreviation for *Ladies Love Cool James.*

BEST LOCATION TO SIT AND WATCH THE TIDE ROLL AWAY, WASTING TIME

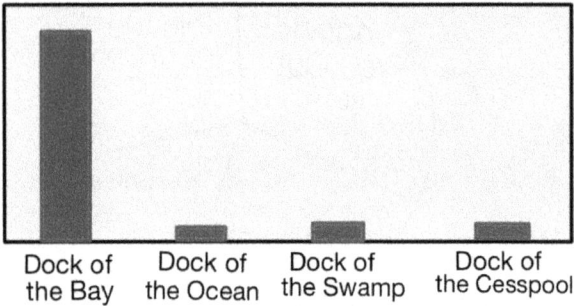

| Dock of the Bay | Dock of the Ocean | Dock of the Swamp | Dock of the Cesspool |

Source: Otis Redding

That guy has been sitting on the dock of the bay since early morning, and now evening has come and he's still there. Somebody should go check on him and make sure he didn't die on the dock of the bay.

When She Is A Woman (To Me)

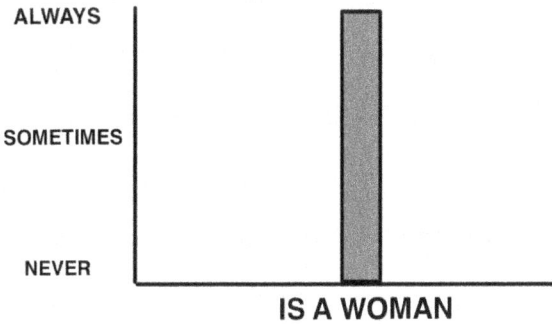

ALWAYS	
SOMETIMES	
NEVER	

IS A WOMAN

Source: Billy Joel

Having two first names can be confusing at an Alcoholics Anonymous meeting.

How Many of Us Can Make It If We Try

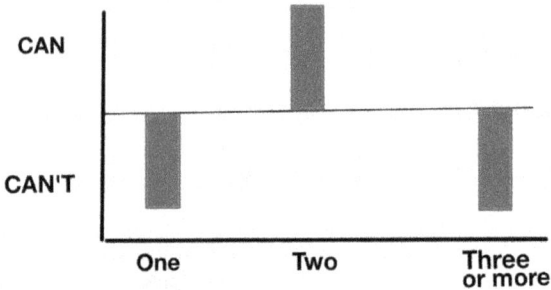

Source: Grover Washington, Jr. and Bill Withers

I'm kind of lazy. Do you think we could make it even if we didn't try?

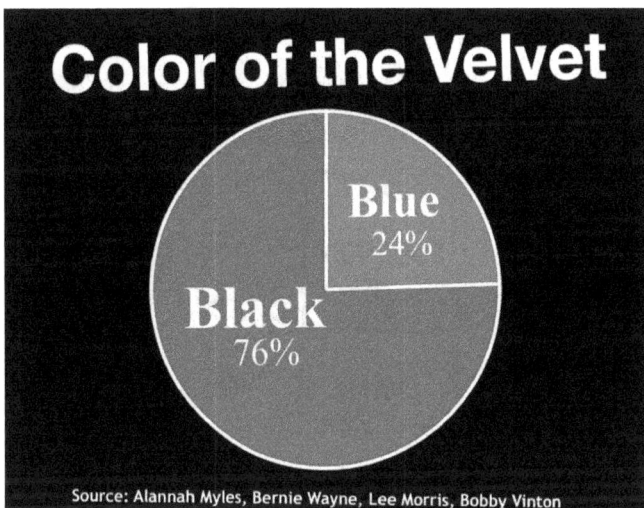

Color of the Velvet

Blue 24%

Black 76%

Source: Alannah Myles, Bernie Wayne, Lee Morris, Bobby Vinton

Velvet is one of the most popular fabrics in song.

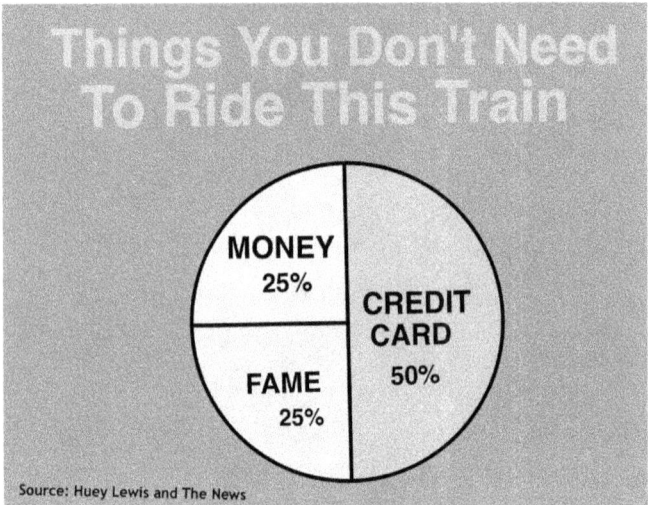

Things You Don't Need To Ride This Train

MONEY
25%

CREDIT CARD
50%

FAME
25%

Source: Huey Lewis and The News

High-speed rail is an environmentally friendly alternative to air travel.

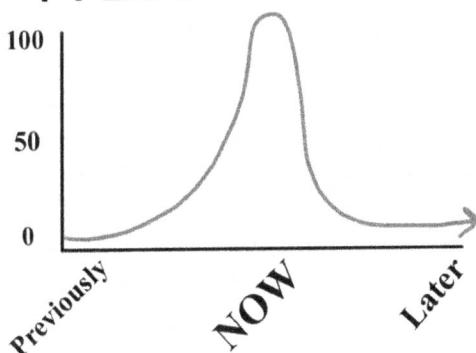

Best Time To Take A Look At Me

100

50

0

Previously

NOW

Later

Source: Phil Collins

Phil Collins was originally the drummer for the band Gene-sis. He took over vocal duties after previous singer Peter Gabriel left. Phil was later replaced by some other guy whose name I forgot to look up.

How Charmed Is This Kind of Life

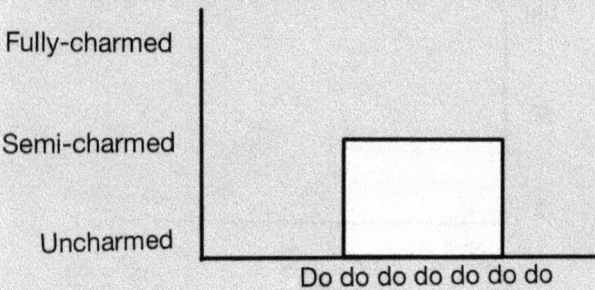

Fully-charmed	
Semi-charmed	
Uncharmed	

Do do do do do do do

Source: Third Eye Blind

If you don't stop singing this song, I'm going to step up on that ledge my friend.

Who I'm Dancing With

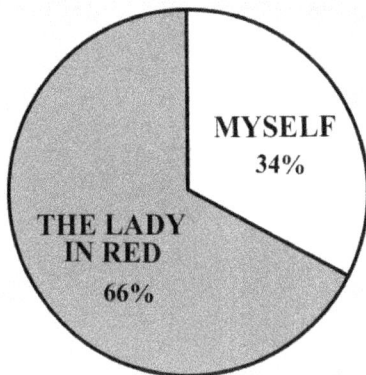

MYSELF
34%

THE LADY
IN RED
66%

Source: Chris de Burgh, Billy Idol

I was dancing with the lady in red, but it seemed like she had never danced before, so I ditched her and now I'm dancing with myself.

BODY PARTS SHE'S GOT

1. Legs

Source: ZZ Top

ZZ Top's anti-amputee views are pretty disgusting.

Who Are the World?

We
100%

Source: USA for Africa

The success of this song allowed Africa to permanently end famine.

How Fast Can Sammy Hagar Drive?

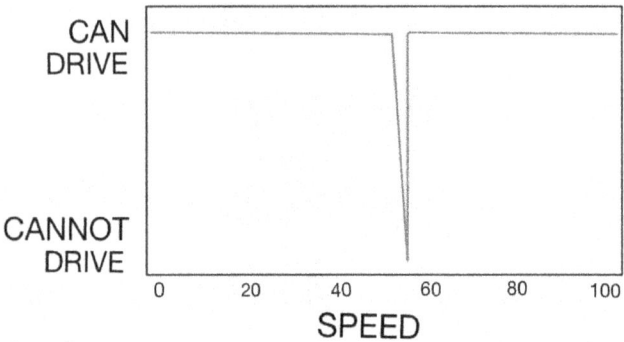

Source: Sammy Hagar

Sammy Hagar's impaired ability to drive is probably a result of him being abducted by aliens, which you can read about in his autobiography.

What is a highway?

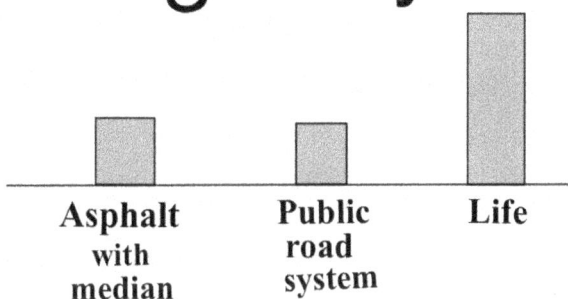

| Asphalt with median | Public road system | Life |

Source: Tom Cochrane

Tom Cochrane got so excited when he first heard about metaphors that he wrote this song.

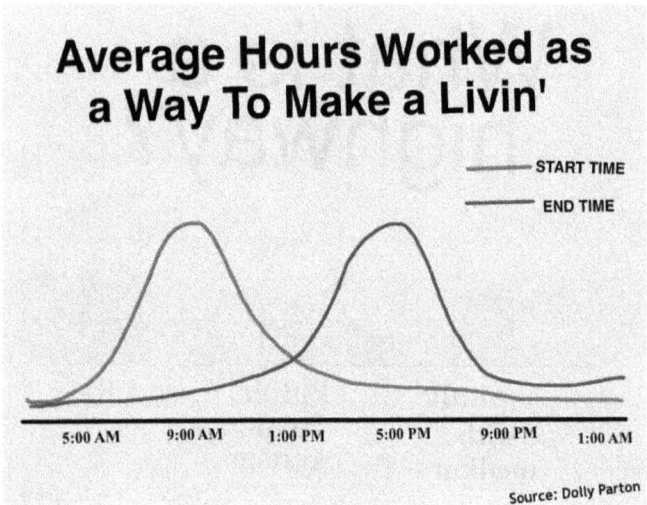

Man, check out the curves on that graph.

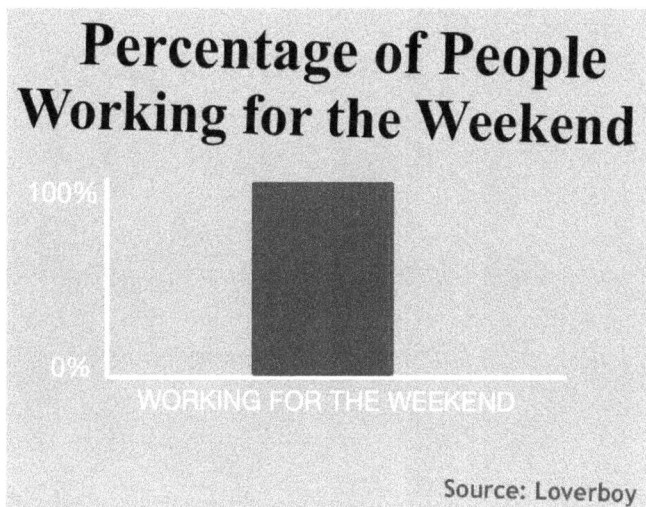

Percentage of People Working for the Weekend

100%

0%

WORKING FOR THE WEEKEND

Source: Loverboy

Weekends didn't really exist until 1940.

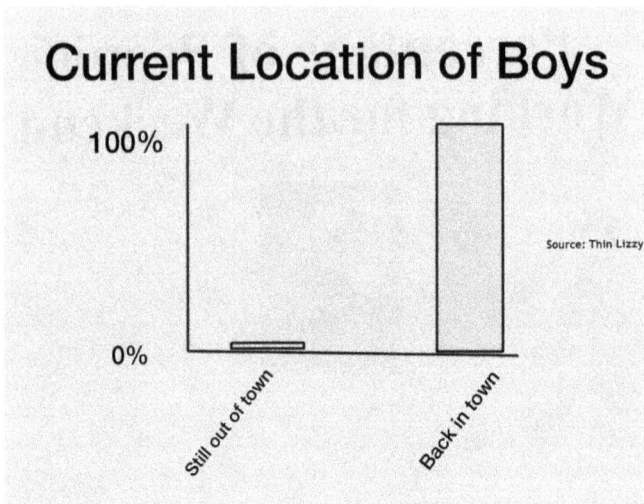

Current Location of Boys

100%

0%

Still out of town

Back in town

Source: Thin Lizzy

Dear Penthouse Forum,

I never thought it would happen to me, but last week I ended up in a town where I was the only boy. It seems that all the other boys had left town, leaving me alone with the sex-starved women. I hope those boys never come back to town, as I am enjoying an orgy like no other ...

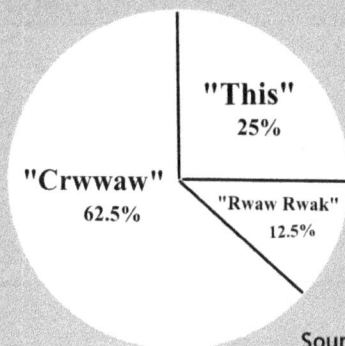

What did you do to the doves to make them cry, Prince?

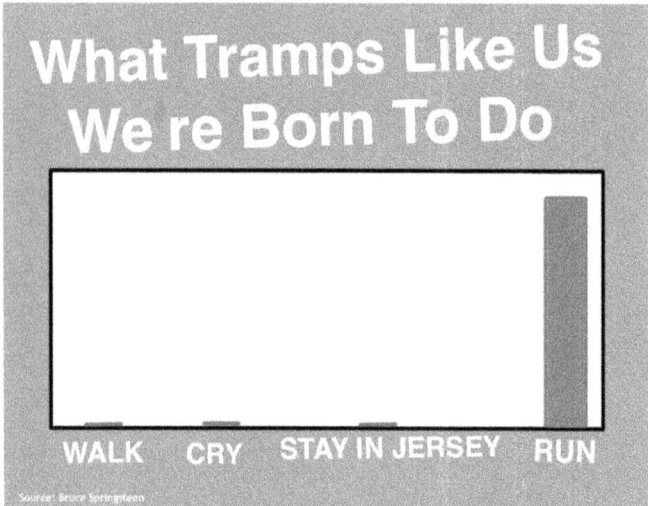

What Tramps Like Us
We re Born To Do

WALK   CRY   STAY IN JERSEY   RUN

Source: Bruce Springsteen

"Tramp" as a verb is a synonym for walk, so it's weird that tramps would be born to run.

Amount of Moisture at Levee
Measured Against Chevy Placement

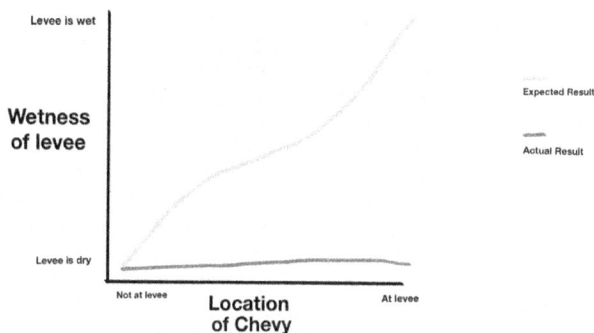

Levee is wet

**Wetness
of levee**

Levee is dry

Not at levee

**Location
of Chevy**

At levee

Expected Result

Actual Result

Source: Don McLean

Don McLean spends a suspicious amount of time down at the levee. What do you think he's doing there?

I read the news everyday, but don't feel the need to brag about it like it's an accomplishment.

Causes of Death for the Radio Star

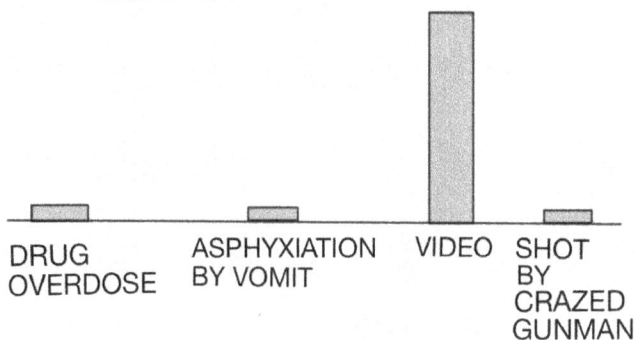

DRUG OVERDOSE | ASPHYXIATION BY VOMIT | VIDEO | SHOT BY CRAZED GUNMAN

Source: The Buggles

One day, holograms will kill the video stars.

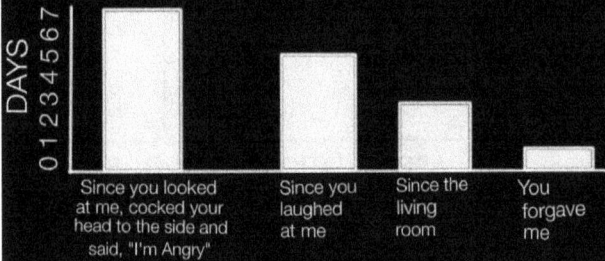

In Canada, this passes for rap.

Analysis of Who Keeps on Fighting

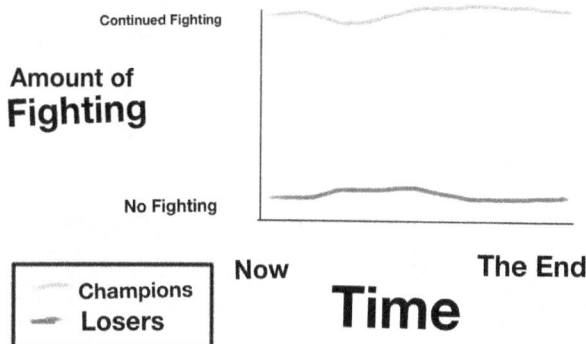

Continued Fighting

Amount of
Fighting

No Fighting

| | Champions |
| | Losers |

Now

Time

The End

Source: Queen

Nothing anybody does will ever be as good as Queen's performance at Live Aid.

HOW WE FELT
ABOUT THE FILM
BREAKFAST AT TIFFANY'S

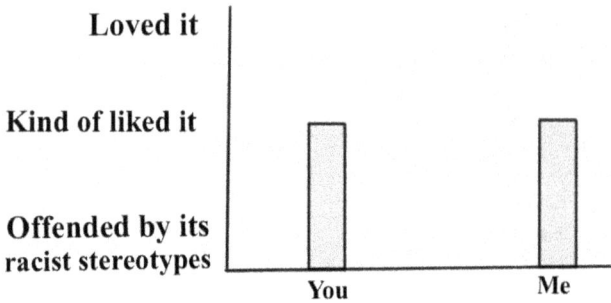

Loved it

Kind of liked it

Offended by its
racist stereotypes

You   Me

Source: Deep Blue Something

Fuck Mickey Rooney.

Amount of Apologies

APOLOGIES
100%

Source: Nirvana

But did he apologize a trillion times?

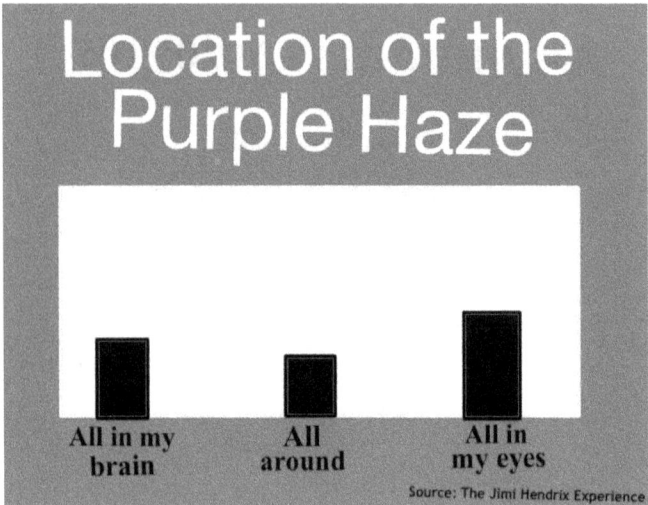

There's a good chance this "haze" is just drugs.

Events That Have Not Occurred in a Long, Lonely Lonely Time

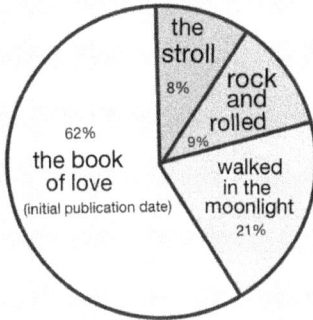

Source: Led Zeppelin

Led Zeppelin may have been involved in a notorious "mud-shark incident" in Seattle, Washington during the height of their fame, in which a woman was sexually assaulted with a fish. The craziest part of the story, though, is that the manger of the band Vanilla Fudge, who possibly has a Super 8 recording of the event, is named *Bruce Wayne*.

APPROPRIATE PLACES
TO BUST A MOVE

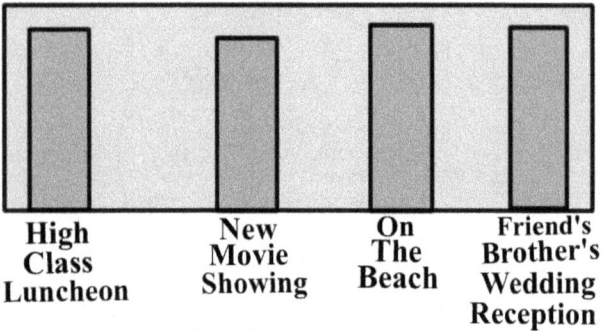

| High Class Luncheon | New Movie Showing | On The Beach | Friend's Brother's Wedding Reception |

Source: Young MC

At the time this song was released in 1989, seeing a movie only cost $5.

Order of Steps for Working It

1. Put thing down

2. Flip it

3. Reverse it

Sources: Missy Elliott, Timbaland

"Misdemeanor" sounds like a badass nickname at first, but is actually rather polite.

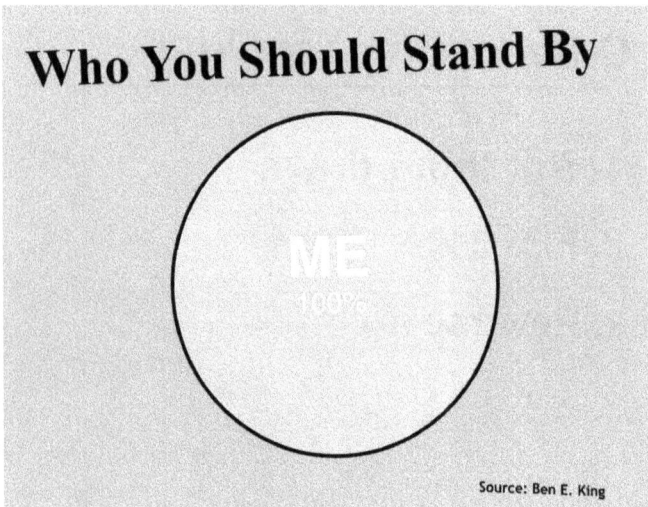

Who You Should Stand By

ME
100%

Source: Ben E. King

Standing by me is a gateway to leaning on me.

When You Will Know Me If You Don't Know Me By Now

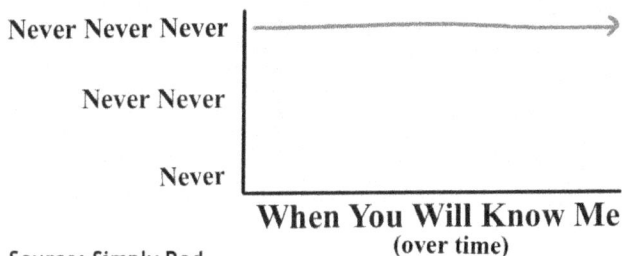

Never Never Never	
Never Never	
Never	

When You Will Know Me
(over time)

Source: Simply Red

You're not that hard to know, Simply Red. Otherwise you'd be Complicatedly Red.

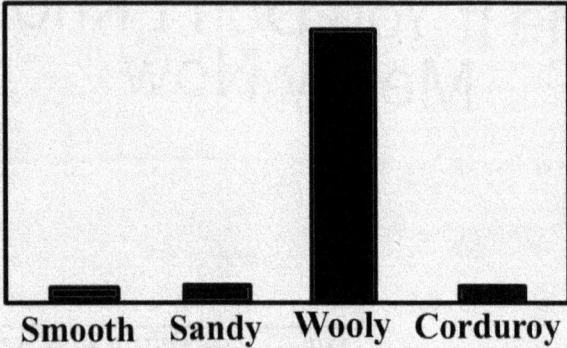

Texture of the Bully

| Smooth | Sandy | Wooly | Corduroy |

Source: Sam the Sham and The Pharoahs

The count-off at the start of this song is bilingual.

WHAT I WANT
THAT JESSE HAS

Source: Rick Springfield

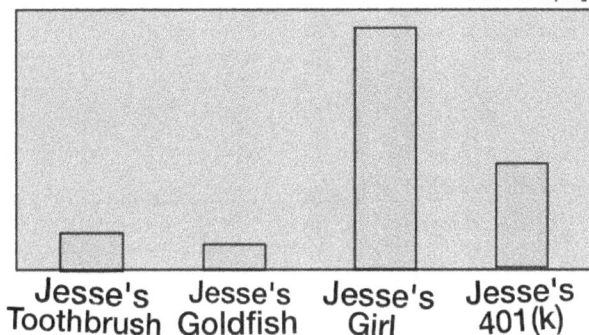

| Jesse's Toothbrush | Jesse's Goldfish | Jesse's Girl | Jesse's 401(k) |

After I first published this chart, I realized that I had spelled "Jessie" wrong. In my defense, Jesse is a more common way to spell that name. Anyway, my apologies to Rck Sprngfeld.

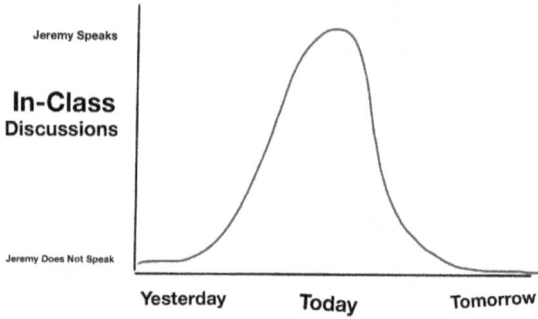

Jeremy's Behavior

Jeremy Speaks

In-Class Discussions

Jeremy Does Not Speak

Yesterday   **Today**   Tomorrow

Source: Pearl Jam

Jeremy's analysis of *The Grapes of Wrath* was kind of anti-climactic after he hadn't spoken all semester.

Who We Should Hear It For

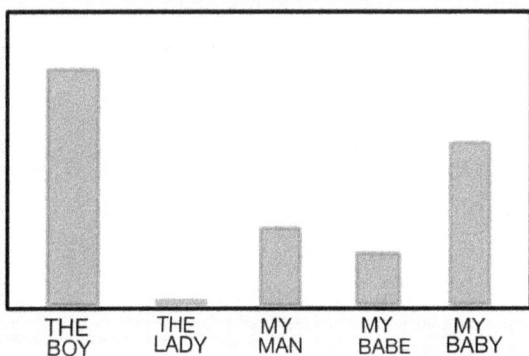

| THE BOY | THE LADY | MY MAN | MY BABE | MY BABY |

Source: Deniece Williams

Why are we talking about the boy like he's not around?

Blood Measurements on a Weekly Basis

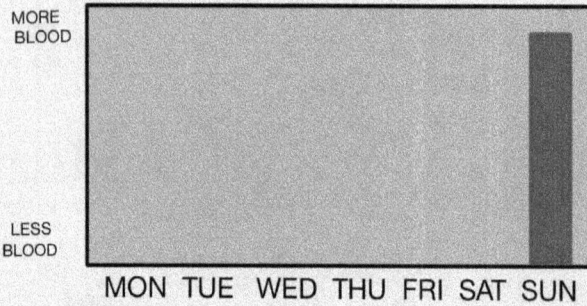

MORE
BLOOD

LESS
BLOOD

MON TUE WED THU FRI SAT SUN

Source: U2

U2 singer Bono has appeared as a talking head in every documentary ever made.

Reasons I Want To Thank You

1. For giving me the best day of my life
2. For being a friend
3. For being Mr. Roboto
4. India, terror, disillusionment, frailty consequence, silence
5. For being kind and generous
6. Falettinme Be Mice Elf Agin

Sources: Dido, The Golden Girls, Styx, Alanis Morissette, Natalie Merchant, Sly and the Family Stone

There are a lot of thank-you songs, but not enough you're-welcome songs.

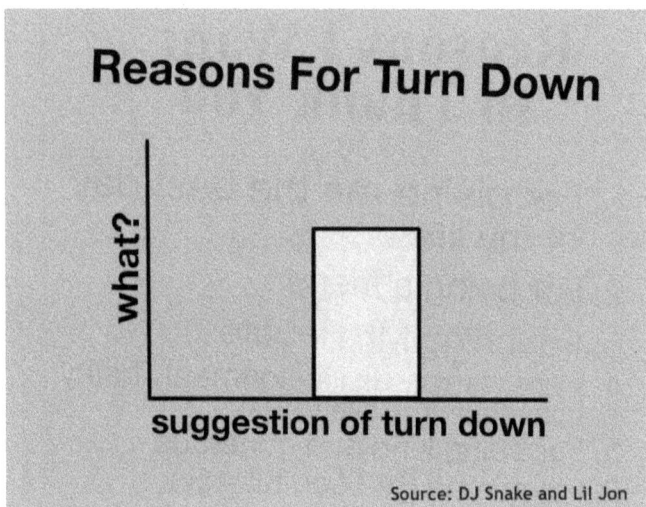

Reasons For Turn Down

y-axis: what?
x-axis: suggestion of turn down

Source: DJ Snake and Lil Jon

A snake is one of the few animals without limbs, which would make it a lousy DJ.

What I Want For Christmas

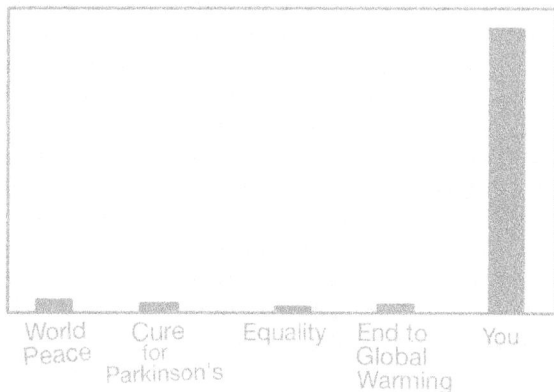

World Peace	Cure for Parkinson's	Equality	End to Global Warming	You

Source: Mariah Carey

All she wants for Christmas is possession of a human being. Is that too much to ask?

NUMBER OF WAYS TO LEAVE YOUR LOVER

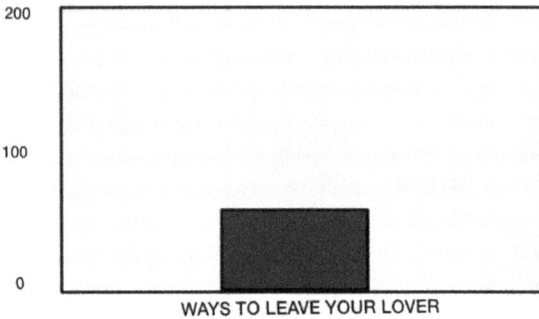

WAYS TO LEAVE YOUR LOVER

Source: Paul Simon

It is easier to leave your lover if your name rhymes with a mode of transportation.

Number of Princes

Source: Spin Doctors

The Spin Doctors had more princes than successful albums.

Acceptable Things

Things I Can't Take Anymore

Joe McCarthy
Richard Nixon
Execution of Ethel and Julius Rosenberg
Hydrogen Bombs
Joseph Stalin's dictatorship
Juan Peron's dictatorship
Soviet violence in Budapest
Violence against blacks in Alabama
Trouble in the Suez
Charles Starkweather's killing spree
Deformed Thalidomide babies
Bay of Pigs invasion   Bigotry at Ole Miss
Assassination of JFK   Watergate
Terror on airlines   Russian invasion of Afghanistan
Heavy metal suicide   Homeless veterans   AIDS epidemic
Hypodermic needles on the shore   China under martial law

Rock and roller cola wars

Source: Billy Joel

Billy Joel is known as the Piano Man by his fans. But also by his enemies, who say it disparagingly, like, "Oh boy, here comes *The Piano Man*. I hope he sings one of his songs about Long Island."

Best Times To Twist

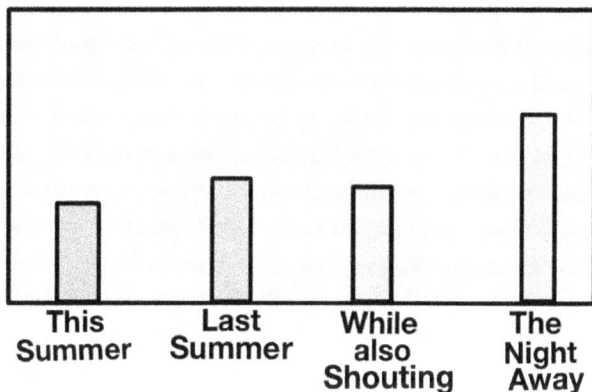

| This Summer | Last Summer | While also Shouting | The Night Away |

Sources: Hank Ballard and the Midnighters, Chubby Checker, The Top Notes/The Isley Brothers, Sam Cooke

Did you know?

Chubby Checker has written and performed a different song about the twist every year since 1960.

2 Chainz and Wiz Kalifa rarely perform together because most theaters do not have enough Zs to advertise their combined names on their marquees.

Things I Want To Do

HAVE SOME FUN
100%

Source: Sheryl Crow

Sheryl Crow once dated bicycle cheat superstar Lance Armstrong.

Things U Can Touch

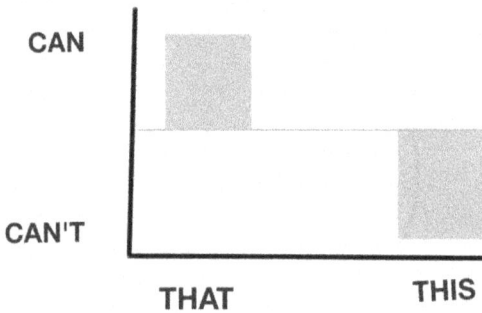

Source: M.C. Hammer

M.C. Hammer is a stage name. His given last name was Escher.

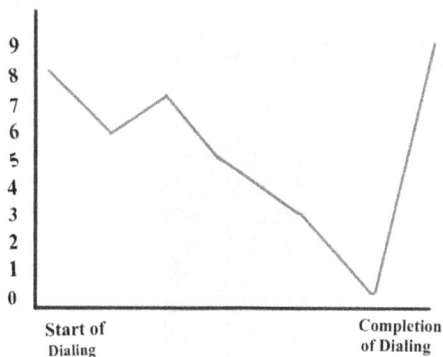

Numbers Pressed While Dialing Jenny

Start of
Dialing

Completion
of Dialing

Source: Tommy Tutone

This is a quaint song about using the telephone to contact someone.

PERCENTAGE OF THE SINGLE LADIES

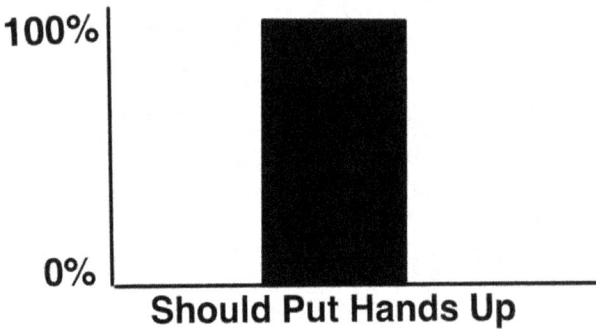

100%

0%

Should Put Hands Up

Sources: Beyonce, Christopher Stewart, Terius Nash, Thaddis Harrell

Beyonce is married to Jay Z, but I think Sasha Fierce is still single.

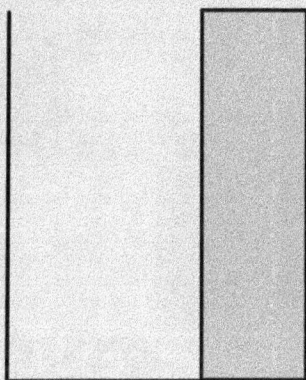

Counting Crows singer Adam Duritz dated the entire cast of "Friends," except for Elliott Gould.

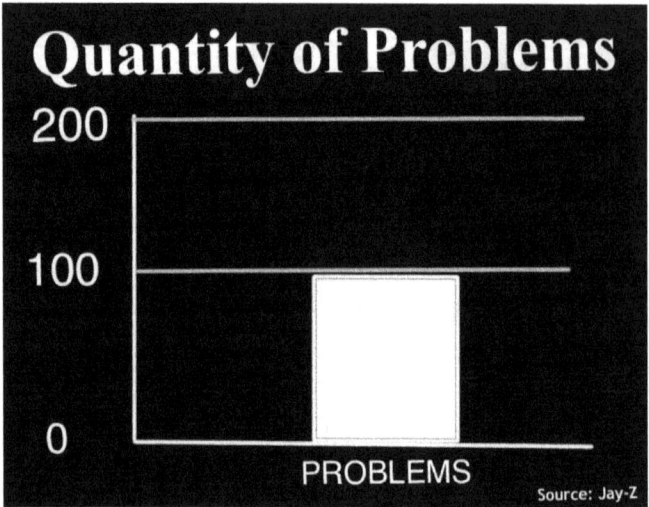

Having 99 problems is almost as scary as having 99 balloons.

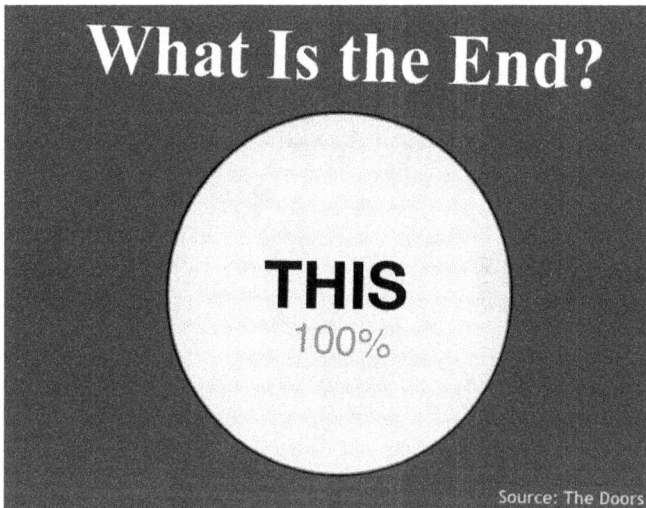

What Is the End?

THIS
100%

Source: The Doors

The Doors were named after a book by home-improvement guru Aldous Huxley.

WHAT HAPPENED UNDER THE BRIDGE

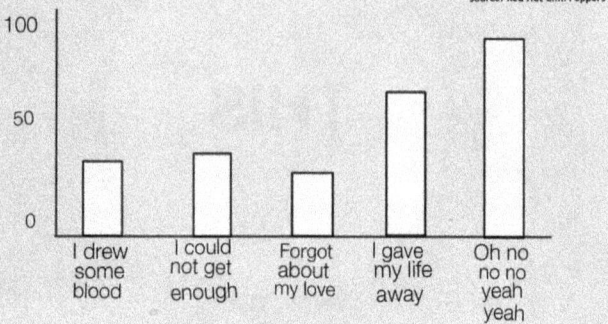

Source: Red Hot Chili Peppers

	100
	50
	0

| I drew some blood | I could not get enough | Forgot about my love | I gave my life away | Oh no no no yeah yeah |

Did you know?

The music video for "Under the Bridge" by the Red Hot Chili Peppers was directed by Alfred Hitchcock.

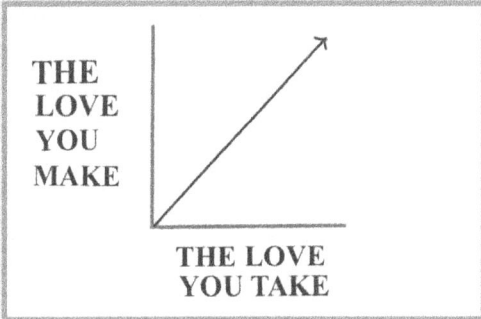

Quantity of Love

THE LOVE YOU MAKE

THE LOVE YOU TAKE

Source: The Beatles

INDEX

INDEX

#

2 Legit 2 Quit, 111
9 to 5, 132
50 Ways to Leave Your Lover, 158
99 Luftballons, 99
99 Problems, 168
99 Red Balloons, 99
867-5309 (Jenny), 165
1999, 61

A

Addicted to Love, 116
Against All Odds (Take a Look at Me
     Now), 125
All Along the Watchtower, 102
All Apologies, 143
All I Wanna Do, 163
All I Want for Christmas Is You, 157
All Shook Up, 81
All Star, 38
American Pie, 137
Another Brick in the Wall (Part 2), 50

B

Baba O'Riley, 90
Bad, Bad Leroy Brown, 64
Bad to the Bone, 3
Because the Night, 2
Best Song Ever, 112
Birdhouse in Your Soul, 41
Black Velvet, 123
Blue Velvet, 123
Born to Run, 136
Boys Are Back in Town, The, 134
Breakfast at Tiffany's, 142
Bridge Over Troubled Water, 118
Bust a Move, 146
Butt, Da, 66

C

California Dreamin', 44
Candle in the Wind, 43
Come On Eileen, 1
Creep, 49

D

Da Butt, 66
Dancing with Myself, 127
Day in the Life, A, 138
Dock of the Bay, (Sittin' On) The, 120
Don't Stop Me Now, 63
Down on the Corner, 86
Dude (Looks Like a Lady), 27

E

Eight Days a Week, 69
End, The (The Beatles), 171
End, The (The Doors), 169
Everybody Wants To Rule the World, 70
(Everything I Do) I Do It For You, 42
Eye of the Tiger, 65

F

Fight For Your Right (To Party!), (You
     Gotta), 53
Fire and Rain, 94
Footloose, 11
For Those About to Rock (We Salute
     You), 108
Free Falling, 31
Fuck Tha Police, 117

G

Get Lucky, 73
Ghostbusters, 103
Girl on Fire, 85
Girls Just Want to Have Fun, 119
Give Up the Funk (Tear the Roof off the
     Sucker), 88
Good Vibrations, 84
Groove Is In The Heart, 10

H

Here Comes the Hotstepper, 54
Hey Jealousy, 109
Hey, Soul Sister, 22
Horse with No Name, A, 55
Hungry Like the Wolf, 95

I

I Can't Drive 55, 130
I Do It For You, (Everything I Do), 42
I Saw Her Standing There, 13
I'm Gonna Be (500 Miles), 51
I'm on Fire, 85
(I've Had) The Time of My Life, 37
If You Don't Know Me by Now, 149
In Your Eyes, 71
Insane in the Brain, 24
It's Raining Men, 6
It's the End of the World As We Know It
      (And I Feel Fine), 104

J

Jack and Diane, 46
Jealous Guy, 100
Jenny (867-5309), 165
Jeremy, 152
Jessie's Girl, 151
Joy to the World, 83
Jumper, 72
Just the Two of Us, 122

K

Karma Chameleon, 107
Kind & Generous, 155
Kung Fu Fighting, 76

L

Lady in Red, The, 127
Layla, 58
Lean on Me, 28
Legs, 128
Leaving on a Jet Plane, 57
Let's Get It On, 16
Let's Hear It for the Boy, 153
Let's Twist Again, 161
Life Is a Highway, 131
Light My Fire, 74
Like a Virgin, 56
Little Red Corvette, 36
London Calling, 96
London's Burning, 96
Love Is a Battlefield, 105
Love Shack, 88

M

Mama Said Knock You Out, 119
Mama Told Me (Not to Come), 119
Maniac, 14
Maps, 32
Message, The, 26
Miss You Like Crazy, 101
Miss You Much, 101
Modern Love, 48
Monster Mash, 80
Mr. Roboto, 155
Ms. Jackson, 9
My Heart Will Go On, 52

N

Norwegian Wood (This Bird Has Flown),
      20

O

O-o-h Child, 45
One Week, 140

P

Party All the Time, 61
Party Hard, 61
Party in the U.S.A., 61
Pour Some Sugar on Me, 7
Power of Love, The, 124
Purple Haze, 144

R

Rainbow Connection, The, 34
Red Red Wine, 40
Rehab, 67
Revolution Will Not Be Televised, The, 62
Rock and Roll, 145
Rock Lobster, 30
Rock You Like a Hurricane, 15
Roof Is on Fire, The, 88
Round Here, 167
Rude, 8
Runnin' with the Devil, 33

S

Scenes from an Italian Restaurant, 47
See You Again, 60
Semi-Charmed Life, 126
Sex and Candy, 17
She's Always a Woman, 121
She's Like the Wind, 23
Shop Around, 119
Single Ladies (Put a Ring on It), 166
(Sittin' On) The Dock of the Bay, 120
Smoke Gets in Your Eyes, 71
Smooth, 115
Son of a Preacher Man, 89
Soul Brother, 22
Space Oddity, 92
Stand, 25
Stand By Me, 148
Sunday Bloody Sunday, 154
Sunglasses at Night, 106
Sweet Caroline, 29
Sweet Dreams (Are Made of This), 18

T

(Take a Look at Me Now), Against All
    Odds, 125
Take On Me, 19
Tear the Roof off the Sucker (Give Up the
    Funk), 88
Thank U, 155
Thank You, 155
Thank You (Falettinme Be Mice Elf
    Again), 155
Thank You for Being a Friend, 155
These Boots Are Made For Walkin', 82
This Land Is Your Land, 12
Time of My Life, (I've Had) The, 37
Tiny Dancer, 77
Truckin', 110
Tubthumping, 93
Turn Down for What, 156
Twist, The, 161
Twist and Shout, 161
Twistin' the Night Away, 161
Two Princes, 159

U

U Can't Touch This, 164
Under the Bridge, 170
Uptown Funk, 59
Uptown Girl, 59

V

Video Killed the Radio Star, 139

W

Wake Me Up Before You Go-Go, 97
Walk on the Wild Side, 4
Walk This Way, 75
Wanna Be Startin' Somethin', 68
Wanted Dead or Alive, 55
Waterfalls, 39
We Are the Champions, 141
We Are the World, 129
We Are Young, 105
We Didn't Start the Fire, 160
We Own It, 162
Werewolves of London, 5
(What A) Wonderful World, 78
When Doves Cry, 135
Where It's At, 98
Wild Side, 4
Wild Wild West, 79
Wild, Wild West, 79
Wonderful Tonight, 91
Wonderful World, 78
Won't Get Fooled Again, 113
Wooly Bully, 150
Work It, 147
Working for the Weekend, 133

Y

Yellow, 114
Yellow Submarine, 35
You Give Love a Bad Name, 21
(You Gotta) Fight for Your Right (To
    Party!), 53
You're So Vain, 87

ABOUT THE AUTHOR

Erik Tanouye is a half-Japanese comedy writer and performer in New York City. Before the pandemic of 2020, he performed to sold-out crowds every Saturday night as part of *The Curfew*. His other books include the novels *The Lovely Breeze* and *A Fake Museum*. He is originally from Maryland.

You can find him on social media at @toyns

www.ingramcontent.com/pod-product-compliance
Lightning Source LLC
Chambersburg PA
CBHW071531040426
42452CB00008B/969